Everyday Life: COLONIAL TIMES

WALTER A. HAZEN

Good Year Books

Parsippany, New Jersey

Photo Credits

Unless otherwise acknowledged, all photographs are the property of Scott, Foresman and Company. Page abbreviations are as follows: (T)top, (C)center, (B)bottom, (L)left, (R)right.

Front cover(l) hornbook, New York Public Library, Astor, Lenox, and Tilden Foundations, Hand-colored for Good Year Books by Cheryl Kucharzak

Front cover(r) Attributed to the Freake-Gibbs Painter, "The Mason Children: David, Joanna, and Abigail," 1670, Fine Arts Museum of San Francisco, Gift of Mr. & Mrs. John D. Rockefeller 3rd, 1979.7.3

6 Philadelphia Museum of Art, Photo by Alfred J. Wyatt

7 Goodwin Memorial Library, Hadley Historical Society, Inc., Hadley, MA

8 Corbis/Bettmann

14, 16(t), 24(all), 25, 33, 46, 55, 56, 63, 64, 65, 66(b), 87, 88 Copyright ©1957 by Edwin Tunis

15 Library of Congress

16(b) A. H. Robins Co.

17 David M. Doody/New York Times

22 Corbis/Bettmann

30 Stock Montage, Inc.

37, 38, 39 Culver Pictures Inc.

45 New-York Historical Society

47 Corbis/Bettmann

48(t) New York Public Library, Astor, Lenox, and Tilden Foundations

48(b) from A LITTLE PRETTY POCKETBOOK, 1787

49, 54 New York Public Library, Astor, Lenox and Tilden Foundations

57 Corbis/Bettmann

66(t) American Antiquarian Society

72, 73 Corbis/Bettmann

79 Ashmolean Museum, Oxford, England

80 Bettmann Archive

81 Culver Pictures Inc.

82 Biblioteca Medicea Laurenziana

86 Brown Brothers

To Martha, Jordan, and Allison

Good Year Books

are available for most basic curriculum subjects plus many enrichment areas. For more Good Year Books, contact your local bookseller or educational dealer. For a complete catalog with information about other Good Year Books, please write:

Good Year Books
An imprint of Pearson Learning
299 Jefferson Road, P.O. Box 480
Parsippany, New Jersey 07054-0480
www.pearsonlearning.com
1-800-321-3106

Design: Christine Ronan Design

Unless otherwise acknowledged, all illustrations are by Joe Rogers.

Copyright © 1997 Walter A. Hazen.

All Rights Reserved.

Printed in the United States of America.

ISBN 0-673-36322-8

8 - BI - 04 03 02

Table of Contents

From *Everyday Life: Colonial Times*, published by Good Year Books. © 1997 Walter A. Hazen.

Table of Contents *continued*

From *Everyday Life: Colonial Times*, published by Good Year Books. © 1997 Walter A. Hazen.

Introduction

Life in the thirteen colonies was difficult. Those early settlers who arrived in America suffered many hardships. They had to endure hard work, starvation, sickness, a harsh climate, and sometimes hostile neighbors. The weak did not survive. The strong who did went on to establish the foundation of what became the United States of America.

In *Everyday Life: Colonial Times,* you will survey every aspect of colonial life. You will see how families were close-knit and had to work together just to survive. You will learn about their customs and their views about life. You will enter their homes and see what foods they ate and what kinds of clothing they wore. You will learn about their occupations, their religious views, and their ideas about education. You will enjoy reading about what they did for fun and recreation and how they traveled from place to place in an age of virtually no conveniences. Finally, from reading *Everyday Life: Colonial Times,* you should gain a better understanding of the colonists' relationship with the American Indians who lived along the Atlantic seaboard at the time America was founded.

Each chapter of this book is followed by three or four pages of activities. Some test your ability to think creatively; others measure your skills in math, vocabulary, and other classroom areas. There are also numerous arts-and-crafts activities that provide further insight into the colonial way of life. There are even a few puzzles for your enjoyment.

You should find the activities in this book both interesting and challenging.

Walter A. Hazen

CHAPTER 1

Family Life and Customs

Life in colonial times centered on the family. This was especially true during the early days of America. With farms and settlements scattered, people often had contact only with members of their own family.

Families were large and close-knit. Many lived, worked, and played in a cabin or house consisting of just one room. It was important that they got along and that everyone did his or her fair share of the work. Usually they did.

Colonists considered marriage a lifetime commitment and frowned upon divorce. For the most part, couples married young. Life expectancy was short, and adulthood came at an earlier age than today. A boy was considered a man at the age of sixteen. Any girl not married by the age of twenty was considered an old maid.

Colonial courtship as depicted on an 18th century dish by a Pennsylvania Dutch artist.

Customs surrounding courtship were much different in colonial times—some are amusing by our standards. For example, in New England when a young man courted a girl, he could only see her while in the presence of the girl's family. The frustrated suitor and the girl whispered to each other through a courtship stick. This was a hollow, wooden tube about eight feet long with an ear and mouth piece at each end. Any conversation between the two had to be carried on through the stick. You can imagine the good-natured teasing they must have endured at the hands of the girl's younger brothers and sisters!

Wealthy parents arranged marriages for their children so they would marry someone of similar position. Love had little to do with it. The fathers of the girl and the boy agreed upon an acceptable dowry. Those girls who could not come up with a suitable dowry often remained unmarried. In poor families and on the frontier, boys and girls usually chose whom they wanted to marry.

Weddings in New England took place in the church. But in the Middle and Southern colonies, couples usually married at the bride's home. These weddings were festive affairs characterized by much drinking and eating. Guests often came from long distances and stayed for days.

From *Everyday Life: Colonial Times*, published by Good Year Books. © 1997 Walter A. Hazen.

Families considered children a blessing. An old Danish proverb states that "children are the poor man's wealth." This helps explain why families were large. Much work needed to be done both on the farm and in the home. Modern conveniences such as tractors and washing machines did not exist. The more children a family had, the more quickly and easily the many chores were finished.

Parents assigned children tasks when they were quite young. Boys and girls learned to make their own clothes. Children knew how to knit and sew by the age of four. Every little girl produced a sampler showing her skills at needlework. Young girls also helped their mothers cook and keep house. Young boys chopped wood, gathered corn, and fed livestock. There was little time for play.

Half the population of early colonial America was under the age of sixteen. People died young from diseases such as smallpox, measles, scarlet fever, and diphtheria. Children died from colds and influenza as well. Old family Bibles tell us of the grief and heartache that colonial parents suffered each time a child died. Cotton Mather, a famous Massachusetts minister, saw nine of his children die before their second birthday. Records show that many parents outlived all their children. And some women had as many as twenty or more!

With death a common occurrence, funerals were frequent. But funerals were quite different in colonial times. The family of the deceased gave gifts to mourners in attendance. The usual gifts were rings and gloves. Those who were most likely to attend every funeral in a town, such as the pastor, accumulated vast stores of such gifts. A pastor in old Boston received 2,900 pairs of gloves in 32 years. Many of these he sold.

The disciplining of children varied throughout the colonies. In early New England, discipline was strict and sometimes even severe. Life was hard and Puritan parents had little patience for unruly children. Among the Dutch and other settlers in the Middle colonies, discipline was more relaxed, and parents tended to show more affection. In the South, parents left discipline to nannies and tutors.

Girls in colonial times made samplers to learn needlework. On a piece of cloth held in a frame, they embroidered their name, age, and the date the sampler was completed. They might also stitch poems, Bible verses, flowers, or trees.

From *Everyday Life: Colonial Times*, published by Good Year Books. © 1997 Walter A. Hazen.

In New England, the well-known saying "children should be seen and not heard" was the general rule. This was especially true during meals. In some New England homes, children sat and ate with their parents. In many others, children ate while standing. Sometimes they stood at the end of the table where their parents sat. At other times they stood elsewhere. They could not talk during the entire meal and had to be courteous and mannerly. Any child who bit into a portion of bread without breaking it into pieces received a good thrashing. As soon as they finished eating, children excused themselves and left the table.

Discipline extended beyond the family circle. Church leaders in New England selected an official called a tithingman. The tithingman had several jobs. One was to keep people awake during church services. Sermons were long and the backless benches churchgoers sat on were uncomfortable. The tithingman had a long stick with a hard knot on one end. On the other end was a fox tail or a cluster of feathers. If a woman or girl dozed during the service, the tithingman tickled her nose with the fox tail or feathers. If a man or boy nodded for a moment, they may be warned with the soft end or receive a sharp rap on the head with the knobbed end.

A New England tithingman ends the nap of a church sleeper. Services were long, and the tithingman was kept busy keeping people awake.

The tithingman also checked on the study habits and behavior of children in the community. From time to time he appeared unannounced at the door of a home. Woe unto those children who had not learned their religious lessons or who were frolicking and having too much fun! Boisterous behavior was punished. The tithingman could take children out of the home and recommend punishment for the parents.

In spite of the strict discipline, colonial parents truly loved their children. The birth of a child was a joyous occasion. In New England, parents gave special cakes to all who came to see a new baby. In New Amsterdam, Dutch families made decorative pincushions with the child's name spelled out with

From *Everyday Life: Colonial Times*, published by Good Year Books. © 1997 Walter A. Hazen.

pins. They proudly hung these on the front doors of their homes.

The names given to babies are interesting and oftentimes meaningful. Some show the pride parents felt at the birth of a new child. Abigail, which means "father's joy," and Hannah, meaning "grace," are two examples. Parents gave other names associated with certain traits or hoped-for virtues. The more common ones were Hope, Faith, Charity, Joy, Patience, Comfort, and Endurance. Sadly, a few names resulted from some tragic incident. A New England mother whose husband had died in a snowstorm named her little girl Fathergone.

Many names were unusual. Supply, Thanks, Preserved, Unite, Wait, Return, Believe, and Tremble show up in records of the time. And would you believe Waitstill, Hopestill, Silence, and Submit? In other sections of the colonies, biblical names were popular. Sarah, Rebekah, Abraham, Joseph, and Israel were a few.

Not only were families close-knit in colonial times, but towns and communities were as well. People shared and helped each other in times of need. They looked after the sick and the elderly. Neighbor helped neighbor clear land, raise houses and barns, gather crops, and make quilts, soap, and other items of necessity.

But the colonists, especially in the North, could be cool to outsiders. Most towns took steps to discourage newcomers. No townsman could sell his house to an outsider without the consent of the town's inhabitants. Some towns went so far as to disallow the sale or rent of a dwelling to anyone other than a local resident. Residents wishing to entertain a guest from outside the town had to get permission from the authorities. When a stranger entered some communities, he was met by either the sheriff or the tithingman and encouraged to leave.

The opposite was true in the South. Settlements and plantations were so spread out that people were starved for news and information. They welcomed all strangers and went out of their way to be hospitable. Plantation owners often stationed slaves at road crossings and alongside lakes and rivers with invitations for travelers to stay over for a night. Innkeepers complained that such Southern hospitality took away a lot of their business—which it did.

In summary, this chapter points out how the colonists felt about marriage, family life, children, and certain customs. Colonial families were close and strong-willed. It was this strength that saw them through the many hardships of life in early America.

From *Everyday Life: Colonial Times*, published by Good Year Books. © 1997 Walter A. Hazen.

Name _____ Date _____

Finish the Tithingman Story

You have learned that some New England communities had town officers called tithingmen. These officers had wide powers. They could punish anyone whom they considered to be "acting out." They watched people in church, in taverns, and in their homes. They were especially watchful for disorderly children.

With these facts in mind, complete the story that is started for you at right.

<u>The Tithingman Story</u>

William Quincy, a tithingman in Salem, Massachusetts, entered the Bradford home unexpectedly one Sunday afternoon. Mr. and Mrs. Bradford were not home. However, the tithingman was furious to find that the Bradfords' son John and two neighborhood boys were home and were wrestling on the floor, laughing loudly, and upsetting chairs and other household articles.

_____

_____

_____

_____

_____

_____

_____

_____

_____

_____

_____

_____

From *Everyday Life: Colonial Times*, published by Good Year Books. © 1997 Walter A. Hazen.

Name _____ Date _____

Research Six Diseases

People in colonial times died of illnesses that are treatable today. Even the common cold claimed many lives.

Listed at right are six diseases that often swept through the colonies in epidemic proportions. Research their causes, symptoms, and prevention or treatment, and write the information on the chart provided for you.

Common Colonial Illnesses

Disease	Cause	Symptoms	Prevention or Treatment
Typhoid Fever	_____	_____	_____
	_____	_____	_____
	_____	_____	_____
Malaria	_____	_____	_____
	_____	_____	_____
	_____	_____	_____
Smallpox	_____	_____	_____
	_____	_____	_____
	_____	_____	_____
Diphtheria	_____	_____	_____
	_____	_____	_____
	_____	_____	_____
Scarlet Fever	_____	_____	_____
	_____	_____	_____
	_____	_____	_____
Measles	_____	_____	_____
	_____	_____	_____
	_____	_____	_____

From Everyday Life: Colonial Times, published by Good Year Books. © 1997 Walter A. Hazen.

Name _____ Date _____

Distinguish Fact and Opinion

Sometimes people say things they believe to be true. In reality they may be only stating an opinion. It is often difficult to distinguish between opinion and fact.

Carefully read the story at right. Then, on the lines at the bottom of the page, write several statements you think are facts and several which you consider opinions.

Jordan and Allison were having a conversation about everyday life in colonial times. As they talked, they compared colonial families with families today.

"Wow!" exclaimed Allison. "Families back then were certainly large!"

"That's true," replied Jordan. "But everyone got along well and there were never any arguments."

"One thing that strikes me about colonial times," continued Allison, "is that parents cared more for their children than parents do today."

"Well, that may be true," said Jordan, "but parents, especially in New England, were very strict."

"Yes," agreed Allison. "And because of that, children were not very happy in those days."

I think these statements are facts:

_____

_____

_____

_____

I think these statements are opinions:

_____

_____

_____

_____

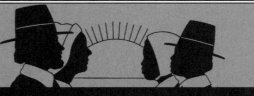

From *Everyday Life: Colonial Times*, published by Good Year Books. © 1997 Walter A. Hazen.

Name _____ Date _____

Make a Pin Cushion

You have learned that Dutch mothers made special pincushions announcing the birth of a baby. The name of the child, and sometimes a short message, was spelled out by the heads of pins. The message might read "Welcome, Little Stranger" or something similar in nature. The pincushions were small, no more than five or six inches long and three or four inches wide. They were usually made of stuffed silk. Sometimes, instead of pins, the baby's name was spelled out in sewn-on steel beads. Many of these pincushions had the shape and design of the one illustrated above.

You can make a similar pincushion by following the directions above.

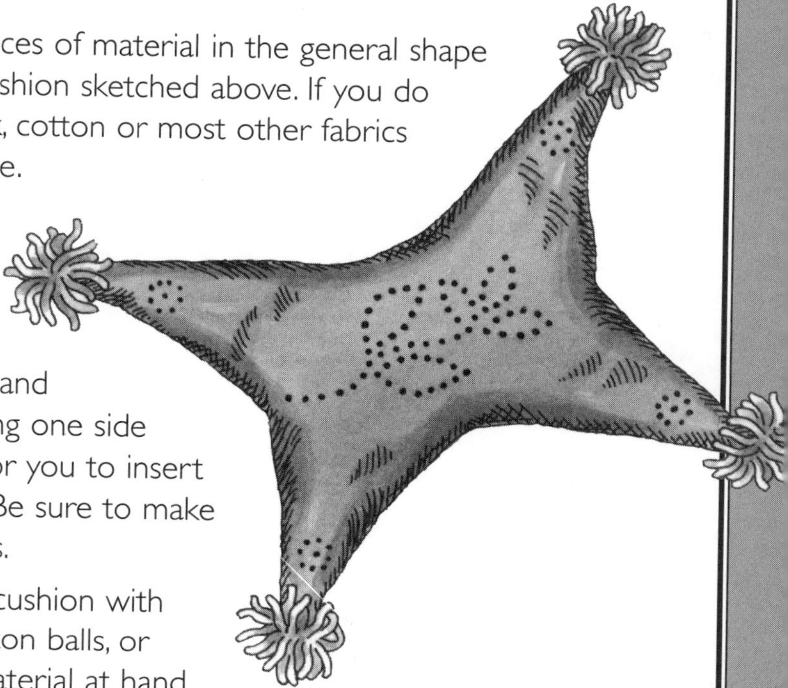

1. Cut two pieces of material in the general shape of the pincushion sketched above. If you do not have silk, cotton or most other fabrics will work fine.

2. Sew three sides of the pincushion together with needle and thread, leaving one side unstitched for you to insert the stuffing. Be sure to make small stitches.

3. Stuff the pincushion with old rags, cotton balls, or any other material at hand. (Colonial women used wool and cotton wadding.)

4. Stitch closed the fourth side of the pincushion.

5. Make tassels or pompons to attach to the four corners in the following manner.

a. Wrap about four yards of white yarn around a flat object measuring several inches in diameter. (A small piece of cardboard will do.)

b. Insert a piece of yarn about six inches long under the yarn you have wrapped around the flat object. Tie a knot in this short piece.

c. On the opposite side from the knot, use scissors to cut through the yarn. Trim the strings to the same length, and you have a perfect tassel. You will need four of these.

d. Sew one tassel to each corner of the pincushion.

e. Use pins to spell out your name with the pin heads.

From *Everyday Life: Colonial Times,* published by Good Year® Books. © 1997 Walter A. Hazen.

CHAPTER 2

Colonial Homes

Did you know that many of the first settlers in America lived in caves? It is true. These early arrivals—mostly men—had neither the time nor the tools to build anything better. This was especially the case in New England, where winters were harsh. Some type of immediate shelter was needed, and caves fulfilled this purpose. These hardy colonists simply dug into the side of a cliff, made a roof of bark supported by poles, and their "castle" was complete!

As conditions improved, more permanent dwellings were possible. Each section of the colonies developed its own style of house, dependent on the climate and the materials at hand.

Drawing of a thatched-roof home typically seen in a New England village in the 17th century

For a while, New Englanders built wigwams similar to those of the American Indians. From these they progressed to box-shaped, wooden houses with thatched roofs. The typical New England house was about 16 feet long and 14 feet wide. It consisted of one long room with a large fireplace at one end. Beams supported a loft reached by a ladder, and this is where the children of the family slept. Floors were either dirt or wood.

Glass windows were rare in early New England houses. Those colonists who possessed such luxuries guarded them at all costs. If they left home for an extended period of time, they removed the panes and took them along. (Iron nails were just as valuable. If a home burned, the owner retrieved the nails from the ashes.) Most homes had windows covered with oiled paper or wooden shutters. This was true well into the eighteenth century in some rural areas.

House-raisings in early New England were popular. They resembled the barn-raisings and husking bees in other parts of the colonies. A group of men and boys could put together an entire house in one day. While this was going on, the women and girls prepared a huge meal that was eaten when all the work was done. In between, there were wrestling and running contests.

Some New England colonists built what were called saltbox houses. They received this name because they resembled the boxes salt was stored in. A saltbox house was one and a half stories high in the front and one story high in the back. It was simpler and less expensive to build than the rectangular wooden house.

From *Everyday Life: Colonial Times*, published by Good Year Books. © 1997 Walter A. Hazen.

Because most early houses in New England were made of wood, fires were frequent. Each family was required to keep several fire buckets near the front door at all times. These buckets were made of heavy leather and were marked with the owner's name or initials. In the event of a fire, each family brought its fire buckets and joined the line attempting to douse the blaze. If, for some reason, people were delayed in hurrying to the fire, they simply threw their buckets outside for others to pick up and use. When the fire was out, individual families identified their buckets by the name or initials written on them.

In the 1700s wealthy colonists in New England began to build large houses of brick or stone. These houses were built in the Georgian style, the style popular in England at the time. They featured gabled roofs and dormers. A dormer is a window that sticks out from a sloping roof. Many of these beautiful houses still stand today. Those built near the coast often had balustrades—railed-in areas—on the roofs called "widow's walks." From these high perches, the wives of sea captains watched and waited for their husbands' ships to come in.

The Georgian-style home of William Byrd in Charles City County, Virginia, which sat on 180,000 acres near the James River.

The Dutch who founded New Netherlands (New York) first lived in dugouts. These resembled the caves used by the early settlers of New England. When they were able to build permanent homes, however, their houses differed greatly from their neighbors to the north.

The Dutch built their houses sideways along the street. The walls at the gabled ends were considerably higher than the roof, which was notched like steps. This was done to prevent chimney fires. Metal gutters extended far out into the street, and anyone passing by during a rainstorm received an impromptu shower.

The Dutch were a social people, and this was reflected in their style of architecture. Each house had a small porch with benches that were in constant use on summer evenings. Also, the front door was divided into halves that opened separately. A Dutch family member could chat for hours through the open top part, leaving the bottom portion closed. This prevented stray animals from entering the house.

Dutch houses had a kitchen separated from the main living area of the house. The primary feature of the kitchen was the fireplace. It was enormous.

From *Everyday Life: Colonial Times*, published by Good Year Books. © 1997 Walter A. Hazen.

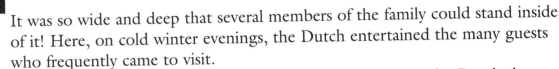

It was so wide and deep that several members of the family could stand inside of it! Here, on cold winter evenings, the Dutch entertained the many guests who frequently came to visit.

No beds were visible in a Dutch home. Did this mean the Dutch slept on the floor? No. Beds were concealed in walls and resembled cupboards. At bedtime, one simply opened the "cupboard," crawled in, and shut the door.

Not all homes in the Middle colonies were as fancy as those of the Dutch. The Swedes and Finns who settled in what is now New Jersey and Delaware lived in log cabins. The Swedes and Finns, in fact, introduced the log cabin to America. This inexpensive type of house later became standard on the frontier. It was also the home built by poorer colonists everywhere.

In Pennsylvania, the Quakers also lived in log cabins at first. Later, in large towns such as Philadelphia, they built beautiful two-story houses of stone. The Quakers were the first to use stoves in America. These were actually ovens with three sides inside the house, and the fourth side, the one with the oven door, located outside the house.

The men who first came to Jamestown were more interested in looking for gold than in building permanent shelters. But the threat of Indian attacks finally led them to build a triangular stockade of upright poles. Inside the stockade they slept in tents and Indian-style wigwams. In the South, the first permanent homes were half-faced camps, which were open on only one side. Later, the typical house in the early days of Jamestown was made of thatch and mud with a hole in the roof for a chimney.

People sometimes think of everyone in the colonial South as living in stately mansions on large plantations. In reality this was the exception rather than the rule. Most Southerners lived in frame houses with chimneys at either end and roofs made of cypress shingles.

But it is for their plantation houses that the colonial South is most remembered. Wealthy planters spared no expense in building and furnishing their homes. Actually, a plantation consisted of a number of houses and buildings. First there was the large mansion with its tall columns and porches—the planter's living quarters. Then there were smaller buildings that served as kitchens, stables, smokehouses, and barns, and possibly a workshop or mill. There were also one-room cabins where slaves lived.

Sketch of a late 17th century Dutch alcove bed. When the doors were closed, the bed completely disappeared into the wall.

An artist's rendition of Jamestown as it looked in 1607. Note the thatch-roofed huts that served as quarters for the settlers.

From *Everyday Life: Colonial Times*, published by Good Year Books. © 1997 Walter A. Hazen.

From *Everyday Life: Colonial Times*, published by Good Year Books. © 1997 Walter A. Hazen.

At first, every colonial family in America made its own furniture. Tables, chairs, stools, and other items were made from log slabs held together with wooden pegs. Later, home furnishings depended on the financial status of the individual colonists. Whether they lived in New England, the Middle colonies, or in the South, those who could afford the expense imported their furniture from Europe. Beautiful tables, chairs, and canopied beds found their way from England into colonial homes. Paintings, carpets, and chandeliers were also characteristic of the more fashionable homes. After a while, colonial craftsmanship progressed to the point that American cabinetmakers began making much of the furniture used in the homes of the wealthy.

In rural areas, it was often possible for a farmer to build his house and stable near a spring. This gave him a ready supply of water for his family and his livestock. But on most farms, and in small towns, it was necessary to dig a well. The well was dug near the kitchen to lessen the distance water had to be carried for cooking. In cities, people got water from public pumps located in the street. Sometimes this water was unfit for drinking and could be used only for washing and cleaning. Street vendors went from house to house selling drinkable water obtained from clear springs.

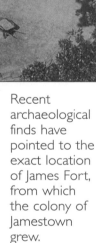

Recent archaeological finds have pointed to the exact location of James Fort, from which the colony of Jamestown grew.

No colonial house had a bathroom. Colonists made do with outhouses located in barns or sheds some distance from the house. In the winter months, they used chamber pots that were emptied daily. Bathing was infrequent, probably done no more than once a month. Often this consisted of washing the hands and face only. Many people thought bathing opened the skin's pores to disease. Submersing the body in water was considered by some to be improper. Several states even tried to pass laws making bathing illegal!

Many homes built during colonial times are still standing today. You can see and visit these houses throughout what used to be the thirteen original colonies. They are a testimony to the skill and craftsmanship of those who built them.

Name _____ Date _____

Prove Your Math Skills

Try the following math problems to test your skill.

1. The early New England frame house measured about 16 feet by 14 feet (4.9m by 4.3m).

   This is about _____ square feet (or meters).

   Find out how many square feet (or meters) your house or apartment contains. Then, using those figures and the figures above for the New England house, write a word problem of your own. Solve it in the space provided below.

2. Colonial families were large and houses crowded. Can you imagine a family of twelve or thirteen living in a one-room house? Some families were even larger. All this meant that the number of people in a town was far greater than the number of houses.

   Study the following figures and answer the questions based on them.

   Colonial town A had 20,000 people living in 3,000 houses.

   Colonial town B had 6,000 people living in 800 houses.

   Colonial town C had 8,000 people living in 1,200 houses.

   Colonial town D had 7,000 people living in 1,300 houses.

   a. Which town had the highest average number of people per house?

      Answer: Town _____

   b. Which town had the lowest average number of people per house?

      Answer: Town _____

   c. Which two towns had the same average?

      Answer: Towns _____ and _____

From *Everyday Life: Colonial Times*, published by Good Year Books. © 1997 Walter A. Hazen.

Name _____ Date _____

Make a Shoebox Diorama

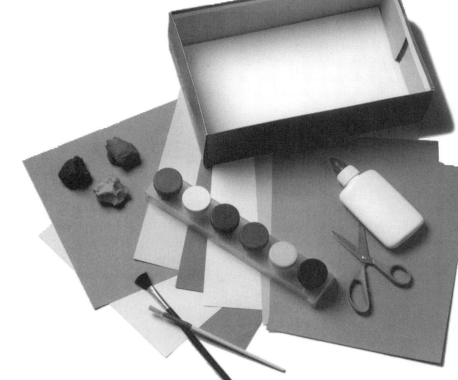

Make a shoebox diorama depicting a scene from everyday life in a colonial home. You might choose to create one of the following scenes.

1. a family eating at the table

2. a woman or young girl of the house sewing, knitting, or spinning wool

3. a meal being prepared over the fireplace

4. a family member reading a book in front of the fireplace

Or, you may want to think of a scene yourself to create.

Some of the materials you will need are

1. a shoebox

2. construction paper

3. magic markers or watercolors and paintbrush

4. glue

5. scissors

6. modeling clay or small figurines

Name _____ Date _____

Home Conveniences: Then and Now

Early colonial homes were sparsely furnished. They contained perhaps a table, some chairs, an assortment of iron pots and wooden dinnerware, several beds, a fireplace, and maybe a cradle. Later homes were more elaborately furnished with products imported from Europe or made by skilled colonial craftsmen. Even so, colonial homes had none of the labor-saving electrical appliances we enjoy today.

On the lines at right, list ten modern conveniences in your home that the colonists did not have. Then, write how you think the colonists made do without such devices.

The first one is done for you.

1. microwave
2. _____
3. _____
4. _____
5. _____
6. _____
7. _____
8. _____
9. _____
10. _____

1. They cooked over an open fireplace.
2. _____
3. _____
4. _____
5. _____
6. _____
7. _____
8. _____
9. _____
10. _____

From *Everyday Life: Colonial Times*, published by Good Year Books. © 1997 Walter A. Hazen.

Name _____ Date _____

Complete a Map of the Thirteen Colonies

There were beautiful homes built throughout the thirteen colonies. Can you label all thirteen colonies on the map?

When you have finished, color each section of the colonies a different color. The New England colonies, for example, you might color blue. The Middle colonies could be colored orange and the Southern colonies, green. You decide the colors yourself.

Make a key for your map in the same colors to show which colonies were included in each section.

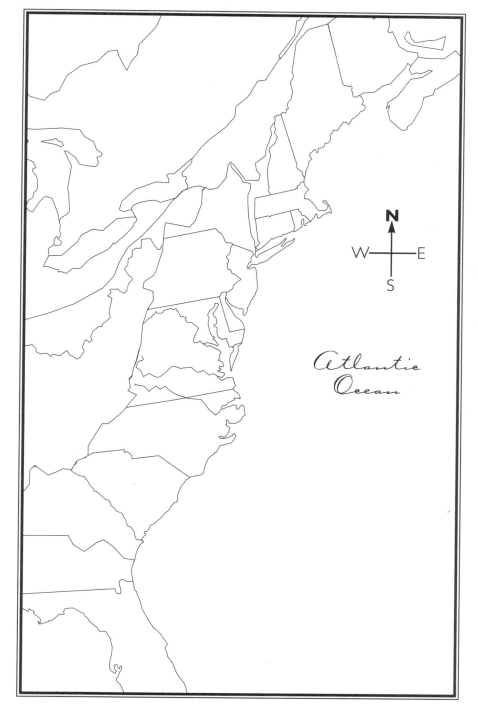

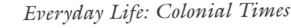

CHAPTER 3

Clothing

The first settlers who came to America gave little thought to clothing. More than half of the one hundred men and four boys who established Jamestown were "landed gentry." Landed gentry were people with the money and the right to own land. Their main interest was in searching for gold. Many came from England dressed in fine clothes with ruffled shirts, while others came with only the clothes on their backs. There are stories of men dying in tattered clothing before any new supplies arrived from England.

Clothing worn by the Puritans was simple homespun and contrasted sharply with that worn elsewhere in the colonies. This scene is from a painting by W. L. Hudson.

Colonial clothing varied from region to region. It was closely linked to religion, social class, and even occupation. The Pilgrims and Puritans in New England dressed very plainly, as did the Quakers in Pennsylvania. Colonists of the Anglican faith in the Southern colonies favored more elaborate styles. The upper classes wore only the finest clothes imported from England. Ministers, especially in New England, preferred simple, homespun suits. Judges wore red robes, while lawyers generally dressed in suits of black velvet.

In early New England, laws forbade everyone except the very wealthy from wearing fancy, imported clothing. The average New Englander had to dress in simple, homemade attire. Anyone dressing otherwise was fined or put in jail. Even the use of buttons was considered too worldly for the Pilgrims and Puritans. They kept their shirts and coats closed with strings.

It is a common belief that the Pilgrims and Puritans only dressed in black and white. This is not true. Although their clothing was plain homespun, the material was often colored with dyes made from roots, berries, and leaves. The usual colors were tan, brown, and russet. (Russet is a yellowish-brown or reddish-brown color.)

From *Everyday Life: Colonial Times*, published by Good Year Books. © 1997 Walter A. Hazen.

Clothing in New England was made from linen, wool, and leather. Linen was spun from the flax plant. Wool was woven from the hair of sheep. And most leather was made from the hides of domesticated animals. Leather was used to make many articles of clothing, such as hats, shoes, and jackets.

New England men wore shirts of linen. A tight-fitting jacket called a doublet was usually worn over the shirt. Long, woolen stockings that came over the knees were tucked under breeches made of leather. High, wide-brimmed hats were worn, although the Pilgrims sometimes wore bright-colored stocking caps while working. On Sundays, some men wore capes and starched collars. Low-cut leather shoes with leather straps completed the men's wardrobe.

The dress of New England women was equally plain. They wore linen blouses and full woolen skirts that came to the ankles. Like the men, they had woolen stockings and leather shoes. Over their blouses they wore a tight bodice, a vest-like garment laced together in front. Over their shoulders they normally wore a white neckcloth. A long white apron and a soft white cap completed their dress. The white apron was especially important. It was scandalous for a girl or woman to be seen without one.

Dress in the Middle colonies was very different. Only the Quakers in Pennsylvania preferred simple clothing. Their clothes were normally of dark and sober colors, with no frills. A few Quakers, however, did not observe such rules of dress. The most prominent was William Penn himself, who founded the Pennsylvania colony in 1681. Penn loved gaily colored, fashionable clothes. His coats were made of silk and velvet. His breeches were made of satin and his stockings of silk. He wore lace collars and cuffs, and sometimes he ventured out with a wide hat decorated with plumes or feathers.

For the average Quaker man, his headgear was his most distinguishing characteristic. He wore a low, wide-brimmed hat that formed a triangle in the front. He seldom removed this important part of his dress. Because he believed all men were equal and no one was superior to anyone else, he never doffed or took off his hat when he passed another person. In fact, a Quaker probably only removed his hat when he went to bed. He always kept it on while indoors—even while eating.

The Dutch in New York placed no restrictions on dress. People generally wore the best they could afford. Dutch women wore wide, full skirts and bodices made of wool or velvet. Around their skirts they wore belts to which they attached such household items as keys and scissors. They covered their

From *Everyday Life: Colonial Times*, published by Good Year Books. © 1997 Walter A. Hazen.

The periwig, worn by Southern plantation owners during colonial times. The prefix *peri* means encircling or surrounding, which it certainly did around the gentleman's head. Our word *wig* is derived from *periwig*.

heads with huge, white bonnets made of linen. Usually, they wore white starched collars. Their shoes were made of leather and had bright silver buckles.

Dutch men wore brightly colored, baggy knee breeches. They had short coats and high, starched white collars. They also wore shoes with silver buckles. Those who could afford them sported large, plumed hats.

Only in the Southern colonies did people try to imitate the styles of Europe. This was especially true in Virginia, where comfort was often sacrificed in the name of fashion. Take the Southern plantation owner, for example. At first he wore his hair in long curls in imitation of the English court. Then he began wearing a periwig, a kind of hairpiece made to resemble naturally long, curly hair. After a while, the periwig was discarded for a regular wig. Most wigs were very expensive, very scratchy, and very hot. They were worn in summer as well as winter. They were tied in the back with brightly colored strings and hung down in a ponytail.

Does the Southern man's wig sound uncomfortable? There is more. The fashion among the wig-wearers was to powder their wigs with white chalk. This practice must have caused no small amount of social embarrassment, as chalk dust often covered the shoulders of the gentleman's coat. Even worse, if a stiff breeze came up while he was on an outing, the unpleasant result was similar to a small dust storm whirling about his head.

The male children of Southern planters also wore wigs on special occasions. Not even the household slaves were spared. At plantation parties, attendees dressed in fancy clothes and wore similar kinds of hairpieces. The same was true of slaves who served as coachmen. Many paintings and sketches from the times show the clothing worn by household slaves on plantations in the South.

A household slave powders his master's wig. Note that the slave is also so adorned. The powdering procedure created quite a dust storm!

The Southern plantation owner completed his dress with satin, knee-length breeches and an embroidered velvet or satin waistcoat. His shirt featured plenty of lace and ruffles, and his coat had gold buttons. If he could afford them, he wore white silk stockings. When he went out, he wore either a cloak or a full-cut coat. His hat kept getting wider and wider, and eventually

From *Everyday Life: Colonial Times*, published by Good Year Books. © 1997 Walter A. Hazen.

he had to pin up one side so he could see. Later he pinned up two other sections of the brim, and the three-cornered hat that became fashionable in the colonies was born.

Southern women were known for their elaborate hoop dresses and skirts. The hoops made a woman's dress stand out four feet on all sides. Special chairs with no arms were necessary just for her to sit down. Beneath the long dress she often wore blue silk stockings and blue satin shoes. Hats were not as important to Southern women as they were to women in the other colonies.

Southern women wore lots of jewelry and always carried a fan. The fan was more than just part of her dress; it could be used as a means of communication. The rate at which a lady fanned herself often conveyed her feelings and emotions.

Typical headgear of a Quaker gentleman. Quakers seldom removed their hats, even indoors.

Some women in the Southern colonies kept patchboxes on their dressers. These boxes, made of silver or ivory, contained tiny "beauty spots" that were applied to the face. Using the small mirror inside the lid of the box, a lady could place the patch in the desired spot on the face or shoulders. You have probably seen movies showing women wearing such patches.

Children throughout the colonies dressed exactly as the adults. Their clothes were miniature versions of their parents'. One notable exception was Dutch children's shoes. Instead of the leather shoes worn by their parents, Dutch children wore wooden shoes like the children of Holland.

Toward the end of the colonial period, dress restrictions were lifted, even in New England. Those who could afford fancy clothes wore them. But clothes could not be too fancy! The song "Yankee Doodle Dandy" refers to overdressed young men as "macaronis." The words to the song vary, but one version goes as follows:

> *Yankee Doodle went to town*
> *Riding on a pony,*
> *Stuck a feather in his hat*
> *And called it macaroni.*

Name _____ Date _____

Try Some "Wig" Math

Thomas Yardley, a wealthy Virginia planter, ordered wigs for his sons Jacob, Samuel, and Adam. The wigs cost 10 British pounds each. Before the wigs arrived, Mr. Yardley had to pay to have the boys' heads shaved. That cost an additional 5 pounds for all three.

Assuming that the British pound is equivalent to $1.60, how much, in U.S. currency…

1. …did one wig cost?

_____

_____

_____

2. …did Mr. Yardley pay for all three wigs?

_____

_____

_____

3. …was Mr. Yardley's total expenditure to outfit his sons in wigs?

_____

_____

_____

From *Everyday Life: Colonial Times*, published by Good Year Books. © 1997 Walter A. Hazen.

Name _____ Date _____

Draw a Picture

Draw a sketch showing the clothing worn by people in one of the sections of the colonies. Look in this chapter, a textbook, or an encyclopedia for illustrations on which to base your drawing.

Name _____ Date _____

Increase Your Fashion Vocabulary

At right are nine words associated with colonial dress. Because they are not normally used in our daily conversations, you may be unfamiliar with some of them.

Look up each word in a dictionary. On the first line next to the word, write its meaning. On the second line, use the word in a sentence.

1. doublet _____

_____

_____

2. breeches _____

_____

_____

3. waistcoat _____

_____

_____

4. stays _____

_____

_____

5. cravat _____

_____

_____

6. neckcloth _____

_____

_____

7. whalebone _____

_____

8. ruff _____

_____

9. petticoat _____

_____

From *Everyday Life: Colonial Times*, published by Good Year Books. © 1997 Walter A. Hazen.

Name _____ Date _____

Create a Colonial Dialogue

Through a time machine, Allison and Jordan are transported back to a plantation in colonial South Carolina. The year is 1725. The scene is a birthday party being given by Mr. and Mrs. Benjamin Pinckney for their eleven-year-old son, Thomas.

Allison and Jordan "crash" the party in clothing typical of late twentieth-century schoolchildren. Both are wearing shorts, T-shirts, and athletic shoes. Young Thomas and his guests are attired in laced shirts, satin knee breeches, and wearing powdered wigs.

Create a dialogue, or conversation, that might have taken place between Allison and Jordan and young Thomas Pinckney and his guests. Continue on a separate sheet of paper if you need more room.

From *Everyday Life: Colonial Times,* published by Good Year Books. © 1997 Walter A. Hazen.

CHAPTER 4

Food and Drink

Regarding food, early settlers in America did not arrive completely empty-handed. They had with them seeds from which they could grow vegetables such as peas, onions, and carrots. They also had brought along a few sheep, chickens, and hogs.

Squanto showing the Pilgrims how to plant corn. A few kernels and a small fish for fertilizer did the trick.

But it was corn that saved the colonists from starvation. Most students are probably familiar with Squanto, the Pawtuxet who taught the Pilgrims how to grow this strange, new grain. Through a series of adventures, Squanto had been to London and could speak English. He met the Pilgrims when they landed in 1621. He and other American Indians taught the new arrivals how to plant corn by placing a few kernels in a hole with a small fish as fertilizer. The Indians showed them when to harvest the crop and how to grind it into meal. Finally, they taught them how to preserve the corn to keep it from spoiling.

Corn became the main part of the diet in all thirteen of the colonies. Most people ate it every day of the year. From corn meal, the colonists made such staples as hasty pudding, which is corn meal boiled in milk. They also made pancakes and johnnycakes. The real name for a johnnycake is "journeycake." It was so-named because it was easy to pack and take along on a trip.

No part of the corn plant was wasted; what did not serve as food was used in other ways. Cattle were fed cornstalks in the winter. Stoppers for bottles and jugs were made from corncobs, as were pipes and handles for small tools. Dolls were often made from the cob of an ear of corn. Corncobs were also cut into pieces and used as checkers. Colonial boys even made darts from corncobs.

From *Everyday Life: Colonial Times*, published by Good Year Books. © 1997 Walter A. Hazen.

Besides corn, the early colonists ate pumpkins, beans, squash, and sweet potatoes. All of these they learned to grow from the Indians. The forests teemed with wild game, so meat was easy to come by. A quick trip to the woods might produce a turkey or pheasant for dinner. Rabbits, geese, pigeons, ducks, and deer were also plentiful. Venison, in fact, was so common that many colonists preferred mutton. Mutton is the meat from sheep.

In addition to meat, the Atlantic coast provided a variety of seafood. Fish was especially popular in New England. Cod, herring, and mackerel were favorites among the Pilgrims and Puritans. Eel, clams, crabs, and oysters were eaten by all the colonists.

Many kinds of fruit grew throughout the colonies. Apples, pears, plums, cherries, peaches, and apricots made tasty pies and puddings. Colonial women also dried fruit for use in the winter months.

No part of the corn plant was wasted. From the Indians, colonists learned to turn corncobs into dolls for little girls.

What was drunk with meals depended on the region. Rum was popular in New England. Cider was the choice of frontier and backwoods families. Those colonists with a cow sometimes drank milk, but milk was usually saved for the making of butter and cheese. In the Middle and Southern colonies, wine and beer were usually found at the dinner table. The College of William and Mary in Williamsburg, Virginia, even had its own brewery and served beer to students in the dining hall. Southern planters and wealthy merchants also had tea, chocolate, and coffee.

It is easy to suppose that the early colonists abused alcohol and drank every chance they got. This was undoubtedly true with some. The truth of the matter, however, is that water was often unfit to drink. In most New England families, everyone had a mug of beer or ale before breakfast, even the children. When these beverages were not available, a family was forced to drink water. Diaries exist in which colonists commented that they had drunk water and survived with no ill effects.

Although there were large skillets for frying and spits for roasting, most meals were cooked in a large iron pot. The one-pot meal became characteristic of the colonies. What found its way into the pot depended on the region.

From *Everyday Life: Colonial Times*, published by Good Year Books. © 1997 Walter A. Hazen.

Several of these meals are still very popular today. One is the New England boiled dinner. It consists of corned beef cooked with cabbage, potatoes, carrots, and onions. Just as popular are Boston baked beans. This tasty dish is made by slowly cooking brown beans with onions, molasses, and salt pork.

No colonists enjoyed eating more than the Dutch. Whatever they ate, they smothered in butter. One of their favorite foods was a waffle made with a long-handled, hinged waffle iron. They also enjoyed cakes, pastries, and olijkoeck, a kind of doughnut filled with raisins, apple, and citron.

Samp porridge was another Dutch staple. It was a type of hasty pudding, or mush, made with meat and vegetables. Samp porridge was cooked slowly in a skillet for three days. When it was done, its crust was so thick that the contents of the skillet could be removed in one large piece. It resembled a pot pie in some ways.

As was explained in Chapter 2, kitchens on Southern plantation homesteads were located in a separate building close to the main house. Wealthier planters built passageways connecting the two buildings, but in most homes, food from the kitchen had to be rushed into the dining area before it became cold.

And what an abundance of food! The well-to-do in the South loaded the table with all kinds of good things to eat. And the food seldom went to waste. Not only were families large, but the frequent guests who came and stayed for days made large meals necessary. It was not uncommon to have platters of pork, beef, game, fish, crabs, and oysters all served at the same time. Add to this hot cornbread and many different kinds of vegetables and you have some idea of the enormity of some Southern dinners.

In spite of the variety of foods mentioned above, the mainstay of the Southern diet was corn. Every plantation had corn fields that produced enough to feed the planter's family and slaves. The plantation owner even made his beer from corn. Corn was also made into a special dish called hominy. Hominy is whole or coarsely ground, hulled corn boiled in water. Sometimes it is fried, and often it is flavored with salt and pepper and butter. Ground hominy is called grits, which is still popular in the South.

Although people awoke and went about their chores much earlier, breakfast throughout the colonies was not eaten until about 10:00 A.M. Dinner, the main meal of the day, was served at 3:30 or 4:00 P.M. A light

From *Everyday Life: Colonial Times*, published by Good Year Books. © 1997 Walter A. Hazen.

meal called supper was eaten just before bedtime at about nine. Southerners referred to the time between dinner and supper as the "evening."

In some colonial families, meals were served in one large pot that was placed on the table, with everyone eating from the one pot. But for the most part, food was eaten from wooden trenchers. A trencher was an early kind of wooden plate. It was a board about 12-inches square that was hollowed out in the middle. All the food was heaped together on a trencher. Children shared one trencher; the parents shared another.

A Puritan family gathers for a meal. Note the absence of forks and the children standing, as children often did at meals.

Since most families did not have forks, food was eaten with the fingers. This required that a satisfactory number of linen napkins be available for every meal. When the meal was finished, napkins, trenchers, mugs, and the like were taken away in a large basket called a voider and washed before the next meal.

As was discussed in Chapter 1, good behavior was expected of children during meals. Rules were especially strict in New England. Children usually ate alone and had to remain absolutely quiet at all times. When they finished eating, they just as quietly excused themselves. After the table was cleared, the mother, father, and older children chatted around the fireplace.

From Everyday Life: Colonial Times, *published by Good Year Books. © 1997 Walter A. Hazen.*

Name _____ Date _____

Make a Colonial Dish

Y̲ou are surely familiar with the following nursery rhyme:

Pease (peas) porridge hot,
Pease porridge cold,
Pease porridge in the pot
Nine days old.
Some like it hot,
Some like it cold,
Some like it in the pot
Nine days old.

The above rhyme tells us several things about colonial cooking. First, people ate porridge, which in those days was a soup made thick by boiling it with flour or meal. Second, food was kept warm over the fire for days. This was the only way colonists could preserve "leftovers" for another meal.

One of the main ingredients in porridge was corn meal. In fact, corn meal was the basis for most colonial dishes. Samp porridge and hasty pudding were two other oft-prepared dishes in which corn meal was the main ingredient. With the colonists eating corn in some form 365 days a year, they tried to use it in as many different ways as possible.

Journeycakes, or johnnycakes, as they came to be called, were also popular. They were similar to pancakes and were often packed and taken on trips. With the help of an adult, you can prepare a meal of journeycakes in about 20 minutes.

Journeycakes

1	cup corn meal
1	cup flour
1	teaspoon salt
1/2	teaspoon baking soda

2	eggs
2	cups milk
2	tablespoons molasses or 1/2 cup sugar

Steps

1. Grease a baking pan with margarine, butter, or vegetable oil.
2. Mix the corn meal, flour, baking soda, and salt together.
3. Add the milk, molasses or sugar, and two beaten eggs, stirring well.
4. Pour the mixture into the baking pan.
5. Bake for 20 minutes at 350° F.

From *Everyday Life: Colonial Times*, published by Good Year Books. © 1997 Walter A. Hazen.

Name _____ Date _____

Find Which Word Does Not Belong

Here are groupings of foods, drinks, and other things that were discussed in Chapter 4. Circle the one item in each group that does not belong. Then, on the line below, explain how it is different from the others.

1.   iron pot   skillet   waffle iron   trencher
_____

2.   pumpkin   corn   sweet potatoes   beans
_____

3.   beer   rum   wine   tea
_____

4.   cod   herring   oysters   mackerel
_____

5.   turkey   rabbit   duck   pigeon
_____

6.   apples   pears   squash   cherries
_____

7.   breakfast   evening   supper   dinner
_____

8.   beef   mutton   pork   crab
_____

9.   butter   molasses   cheese   cream
_____

From Everyday Life: Colonial Times, published by Good Year Books. © 1997 Walter A. Hazen.

Name _____ Date _____

Solve a Food Crossword Puzzle

Solve this crossword puzzle using what you just learned in Chapter 4.

Across

3. _____ pudding

5. A Dutch doughnut

7. _____ porridge

9. A hollowed-out wooden plate

12. Deer meat

Down

1. What the colonists seldom drank

2. Ground hominy

4. It was eaten by all the colonists

6. Meat from sheep

8. A thick soup

10. A kind of fish eaten in New England

11. _____ baked beans

From *Everyday Life: Colonial Times*, published by Good Year Books. © 1997 Walter A. Hazen.

CHAPTER 5

Fun and Amusements

Recreation in colonial America was as varied as the people themselves. Amusements ranged from bowling and horse racing to husking and quilting bees.

In early New England, most kinds of amusement were frowned upon by the Puritan leaders. This was especially true of activities such as dancing and card-playing. So people turned work into play, and husking and quilting bees became popular forms of entertainment.

A quilting bee in western Virginia in the 1850s. Quilting bees changed very little from colonial times. Quilting parties helped turn work into a form of entertainment.

A bee was a gathering of people who made work fun and competitive. Two sides competed to see who could husk or shuck the most corn in a given time, or women raced one another in making quilts. Sometimes a lad who happened upon a red ear of corn won the right to kiss the girl of his choice. Later, the New England colonies became more liberal and tolerated such amusements as cards, dancing, and billiards, or pool. Ice-skating was also popular during the winter months.

Rules were more relaxed in the Middle colonies. Here, people enjoyed horse racing and games such as skittles and bowling. Skittles was an early form of bowling that used nine pins. In fact, it was often called ninepins after being introduced by the Dutch in the seventeenth century. As time went on, colonists began to gamble so much on the game that the colonial government of New York outlawed it. But the clever colonists found a way to get around the law. They added a tenth pin, which, in their way of thinking, made the game "tenpins" instead of ninepins and was therefore perfectly legal!

Horse racing was a favorite of colonists everywhere. It was especially popular in the Middle colonies, where betting on horses was a favorite pastime of the country gentry. New breeds with powerful lungs and strong legs made racing challenging and exciting. Even George Washington himself loved to bet on the races, and his diary tells us that he lost much more than he ever won at the tracks.

From *Everyday Life: Colonial Times*, published by Good Year Books. © 1997 Walter A. Hazen.

Dancing was a favorite form of entertainment in the colonies. Jigs were especially popular in the South. Although this picture dates from the 1850s, it might just as easily have been drawn one hundred years earlier.

As well as horse racing and bowling, people in the Southern colonies enjoyed cockfighting, fox hunting, and gambling. Men and boys came from miles around to watch and bet on races and fights.

But the Old South is most noted for its plantation parties. Because distances between plantations were great and guests came from many miles, these balls often went on for days. One Virginia planter gave a ball that was attended by seventy-five guests and continued—with short intermissions from time to time—for three days and nights. Often a guest would stay for weeks, even months. At these gala affairs, people dressed in elegant clothes and danced the minuet, a graceful dance imported from Europe. They also danced the country jigs for which the South became known.

Nowhere was entertainment more important than on the frontier. Hard-working pioneers needed diversions from the toil and dangers of everyday life. They too relished the husking bees and quilting bees so popular in other areas of colonial America. But they also had their own particular forms of entertainment. Chief among these were footraces and wrestling contests.

Frontier people turned any kind of work into competitive fun. They held barn-raisings and cabin-raisings where men and boys displayed their building skills. They also scheduled stone bees and piling bees. In a stone bee, men raced to see who could remove the largest number of stones or rocks from a field in a given time. A piling bee was a work-play activity involving the removal of tree stumps. Before a piling bee began, the men and boys competed in a chopping bee to recognize a champion at felling trees.

Even colonial barn dances combined play with work. Barn dances were actually called "bran" dances. Before a dance began, kernels of corn were thrown on the rough wood of a newly laid barn floor. While they danced and had fun, the feet of the dancers pressed the oil from the kernels into the raw wood, helping to make it smooth and polished.

A popular game enjoyed by adults throughout the colonies was quoits. A quoit was a metal ring that was tossed at an iron stake driven into the ground. Points were scored by ringing a stake with a quoit or by placing it as close to the stake as possible. Only the wealthy could afford to buy quoits. Other colonists substituted horseshoes and found they worked just fine. That is how the game of horseshoes was passed down to us.

All colonists looked forward to fairs. Fairs provided farmers with a place to sell their produce and have fun at the same time. Families thrilled to races, puppet shows, magicians, animal acts, jugglers, and acrobats. A sketch of the

From *Everyday Life: Colonial Times*, published by Good Year Books. © 1997 Walter A. Hazen.

times shows an acrobat teetering on a wire and balancing a wine goblet on his forehead. Stacked on top of the goblet is a deck of cards, and on top of that a sword. At the same time he is firing a pistol! This may sound a little farfetched, but it gives you an idea of what fair-goers enjoyed.

Fairs also gave men and boys a chance to win a prize by catching a greased pig or by shinnying up a greased pole. Sometimes a goose was greased and hung by its legs from a wire over a pond. A contestant stood on a plank at the stern of a boat and tried to catch the flapping bird as the boat was rowed beneath the wire. Often as not, the prize-seeker could not hold on and was unceremoniously dunked into the pond.

Children throughout the colonies played games with which you are familiar. Hopscotch, leapfrog, marbles, tag, hide-and-seek, and blindman's buff were but a few. They also played board games like checkers and backgammon. Their toys, such as kites and tops, were usually homemade. So too were little girls' dolls. Dolls were made generally from rags, cornhusks, or wood, but sometimes much simpler materials, such as pine cones and corncobs, were used. Girls from wealthy families might be lucky enough to own an imported doll from Europe.

Colonial children playing Blindman's Buff, a game that has carried over to modern times.

Colonial boys also played street games similar to baseball and football. "Football" was brought over from Europe, where it had been played since the Middle Ages. It was such a rough game that many European towns had found it necessary to ban it completely. The game was usually played on cobblestone streets, and too many boys and young men had ended up being maimed for life after being "gang-tackled" on a pile of bricks.

Finally, theaters and concert halls sprang up in cities from Boston, Massachusetts, to Charleston, South Carolina. Those colonists who could afford such entertainment spent many pleasant evenings enjoying their favorite plays and concerts.

Name _____ Date _____

Solve a Word Problem

Husking bees were popular forms of colonial entertainment. Huskers raced in teams to see who could shuck the most corn in a given period of time.

Husking bees served a more practical purpose as well. You are probably familiar with the saying "many hands make light work." This was certainly true during colonial times. People from surrounding farms would gather and help a neighbor bring in and shuck his corn crop. They also raised barns and completed other tasks in the same way. When the work was done, a huge meal was enjoyed by all. The evening almost always ended in a square dance.

Solve the following word problem associated with a husking bee.

Neighbors from all around have gathered at Caleb Wilson's farm to help him shuck his corn. A portion of the crop is divided into two equal piles. A time limit is established, and the race is on!

Group A shucks 350 ears. Group B shucks 8% more than Group A.

How many ears are shucked by Group B?

_____

What was the total number of ears shucked?

_____

From *Everyday Life: Colonial Times*, published by Good Year Books. © 1997 Walter A. Hazen.

Name _____ Date _____

Make a Kite

Kites have been around for a long time. Ancient Asians were making and flying kites before the time of Christ. Even today, Asians continue to be interested in kites. Countries like China and Japan have special holidays when thousands of kites fill the skies over towns and cities.

Colonial children enjoyed kites too. They could hardly wait until spring came to fly them. With rare exceptions, kites were homemade. They were flat, triangular-shaped "two-stickers" made of paper or thin cloth with a tail fashioned from strips of cloth. This simple kind of kite continued to be made at home by children for generations.

With a few simple materials, you can make a kite similar to the ones flown in colonial times. And remember: half the challenge is getting the thing off the ground and into the air!

Ask your Mom or Dad, or a friend or classmate, to help you make your kite. Any encyclopedia will furnish you with simple, easy-to-follow instructions.

Materials you will need include

1. Two thin, rounded sticks—one about 30 inches long and the other about 36 inches

2. A sheet of tissue, crepe, or lightweight gift-wrapping paper to attach to the sticks

3. Glue and string to hold the kite together

4. String to fly the kite

5. A stick to use as a reel

6. Cloth or paper to make a tail

7. Watercolors or poster paint to paint the kite

Name _____ Date _____

Interpret a Line Graph

You have learned that bowling was very popular in the colonies and that at first it was called ninepins.

Ninepins was actually one of several bowling games played by the colonists. Another kind of bowling involved players rolling a larger ball and attempting to stop it as close as possible to a smaller ball resting on the green. The player closest to the target ball was declared the winner. This type of bowling was similar to the modern game of pitching pennies at a line drawn in the dirt. In pitching pennies, the player whose penny is nearest the line wins the game.

At right is a math activity that centers around bowling. It challenges your ability to read a line graph. Although women did not participate in the sport in colonial times, several are included in the graph since many women and girls today enjoy bowling.

A group of young colonists have just completed a spirited game of bowling. The line graph below shows the number of strikes recorded by each bowler during the game.

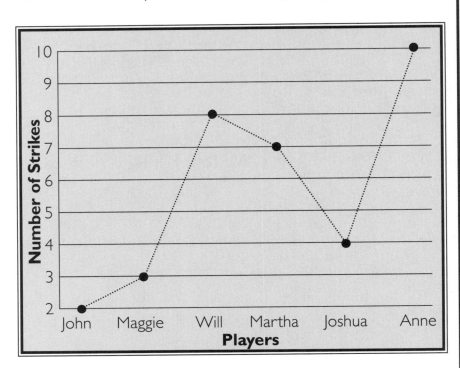

Use the graph to answer these questions:

1. How many strikes did Will have? _____

2. How many more strikes did Martha have than Maggie? _____

3. Who had the highest number of strikes? _____

   Who had the least? _____

4. What was the average number of strikes for the whole group? _____

From *Everyday Life: Colonial Times*, published by Good Year Books. © 1997 Walter A. Hazen.

Name _____ Date _____

Prepare a Time Machine Journal

Imagine that through a time machine, you are whisked back 250 years to a colony of your choice.

Compose a journal describing your experiences. In your journal, include the following:

1. What the people were doing for fun and amusement

2. How their recreational activities compared to ours

3. What you would tell them about forms of entertainment today, and what you think their response might be

Dear Journal,

_____

_____

_____

_____

_____

_____

_____

_____

_____

_____

_____

_____

_____

_____

_____

_____

_____

_____

_____

_____

From *Everyday Life: Colonial Times,* published by Good Year Books. © 1997 Walter A. Hazen.

Name _____ Date _____

Write About Your Leisure Activities

Leisure activities were an important part of colonial life. The same holds true for society today.

Write a short paper explaining why fun and recreation are so important to all of us. Include several reasons in your report.

From *Everyday Life: Colonial Times*, published by Good Year Books. © 1997 Walter A. Hazen.

Religion and Education

When studying religion and education in the colonies, it is best to begin with New England. Nowhere were these issues taken more seriously than in the North.

The Pilgrims were the first settlers in what later became Massachusetts. In England, they were called Separatists because of their break with the Church of England. The Pilgrims were not as strict in their beliefs as the Puritans. The Pilgrims believed everyone had the right to worship as he or she pleased.

Pilgrims on their way to church, from a painting by George Boughton. Why do you suppose the men are carrying guns?

Nine years after the Pilgrims landed at Plymouth, the Puritans arrived and founded the Massachusetts Bay Colony. Their name came from their desire to "purify," or change, the Church of England. To escape punishment in their homeland, they sailed for America in 1630.

The Puritans, ironically, came to America for religious freedom, but they were unwilling to grant this right to others. Anyone who settled in Massachusetts was forced to follow Puritan beliefs. Those who objected were treated harshly. Even gentle Quakers were flogged and sometimes hanged for having different religious opinions.

Everyone in Massachusetts was required to attend church. The few who did not faced severe punishment and loss of their voting rights. Church leaders enjoyed powers unheard of among ministers in the Middle and Southern colonies.

The Puritans made Sunday a day of complete worship. No other kind of activity was permitted. Meals could not be cooked nor houses cleaned on Sunday. Children were not permitted to play. Anyone caught running, jumping, or singing could be fined 40 shillings, a huge sum. No farmer could plow or shop owner do business on Sunday. These Sunday "blue laws" that began in New England continued in some places right up to modern times.

Once at church, the Puritans resigned themselves to a very long day. They had to sit on hard wooden benches through two services. There was a service in the morning and another in the afternoon. Meeting houses, as the

From *Everyday Life: Colonial Times*, published by Good Year Books. © 1997 Walter A. Hazen.

Puritans called their churches, were unheated and extremely uncomfortable in winter. It was so bad that people were permitted to bring their dogs to church to sleep on their feet and keep them warm. But a dog had to be well-behaved. Any dog that acted up was immediately removed by a church official called a dog-pelter or dog-whipper.

Each Puritan service began with a one-hour prayer by the minister. This he followed with a sermon that often lasted four hours. Imagine sitting through two services that might total ten hours! The tithingman and his stick were kept quite busy. (For more on the tithingman, see page 8.)

Puritan justice for lawbreakers was swift. Usually, its purpose was to humiliate the offender. Punishments ranged from the ducking stool for women accused of gossip (see picture, page 52) to the pillory and stocks for other offenses. The pillory held a person's head and arms securely between two planks cut to form holes or openings. The stocks did the same for the feet.

Two men are punished in the manner common in colonial New England. The letters on their persons inform passersby of their wrongdoings.

Both the pillory and the stocks were located on a platform in the village square. Here offenders were jeered at and ridiculed by passers-by. Signs were attached to their bodies with letters indicating their offenses. A drunkard might have a "D" pinned to his shirt, while someone guilty of cursing would wear the letter "B" for blasphemy.

Serious crimes brought severe punishment. Every town had a whipping post that saw plenty of use. Sometimes, unfortunate offenders were branded with hot irons. In extreme cases, ears and hands were cut off to set an example for would-be criminals.

Puritan harshness reached its peak in 1692 with the Salem witch trials. Because of the testimonies of a few young girls, nineteen innocent people were executed for "practicing witchcraft." Later historians claim that Puritan leaders actually staged the trials because they were losing their stronghold on the people.

Superstition and the belief that the devil was everywhere was true to some degree even in the Middle colonies. But there was a much greater measure of religious tolerance in New York, New Jersey, Pennsylvania, and Delaware.

The Dutch in New York belonged to the Dutch Reformed Church. Sunday attendance was encouraged but not forced. There were, however, certain rules of behavior that applied to the Sabbath. No work or games were

From *Everyday Life: Colonial Times*, published by Good Year Books. © 1997 Walter A. Hazen.

permitted, and taverns were expected to stay closed during church hours. Drinking was allowed, but not drunkenness.

The Quakers who settled in Pennsylvania and New Jersey were a unique group. Their real name was the Society of Friends. They were called Quakers because they sometimes shook with emotion during services. They had no pastors, and anyone who felt moved to pray or talk during meetings could. The Quakers believed in true democracy and in the equality of all people. They welcomed people of other faiths in their midst.

Other religious groups flourished in the Middle colonies. There were Anglicans, Presbyterians, Jews, Catholics, and Lutherans, to name a few. In the Southern colonies, the Church of England (Anglican) became the official church. The South was as tolerant as the Middle colonies regarding religion. People of different faiths lived side by side and got along quite well.

As with religion, the people of the Northern colonies placed a high priority on education. In 1636, the Puritans in Massachusetts founded Cambridge College, the first institution of higher learning in America. Cambridge became known as Harvard in 1638.

The first schools in New England for children were called dame schools. The word *dame* as used here refers to a schoolmistress, or teacher. Usually the teacher was an elderly widow. Classes were held in her home, and she often went about her daily chores as the children did their lessons.

Colonial children, not all of them attentive, study their lessons in a New England Dame School. From a 1713 engraving.

The curriculum of a dame school consisted of learning the alphabet, reading, and ciphering. Ciphering was simple arithmetic. To study the alphabet, students used a device known as a hornbook. A hornbook was not a book at all but a flat board with a handle that had lessons attached to its front and back. Some hornbooks were made to resemble frames, and lessons could be slipped in and out and therefore changed frequently. Most hornbooks, however, had a lesson permanently pasted on each side. For example, the type of hornbook used by the dame schools had the alphabet permanently printed on one side, and the Lord's Prayer printed on the other side. To protect the printed paper, a thin, transparent sheet of animal horn was placed over both

From *Everyday Life: Colonial Times*, published by Good Year Books. © 1997 Walter A. Hazen.

A typical hornbook, so named because it had a horn-covered writing surface so that it could be used again and again

sides of the hornbook. Paper was scarce in colonial times, and covering the "book" with horn insured that it could be used year after year.

Education in the dame schools emphasized rote learning. Lessons were repeated over and over again until they were memorized. Oftentimes, these lessons were given in rhyme. Many such rhymes have come down to us through the centuries. One of the more familiar is quoted below.

> *Thirty days hath September,*
> *April, June, and November.*
> *February hath twenty-eight alone,*
> *And all the rest have thirty-one.*

Students attended a dame school for only two years. For many colonial children, that was the end of their education. This was especially true for girls. The Puritan leaders felt that two years of education was all a girl needed. After all, her only option at that time was to work her whole life at the job of wife and mother. Some men believed that too much education caused insanity in girls and women!

Larger New England towns might have "common schools." These schools provided the student with four more years of education. Most common schools were one-room schoolhouses with a fireplace. Students were required to bring firewood every day to keep the fire going. Any student who forgot his or her firewood had to sit in the back of the room where the warmth of the fire never reached.

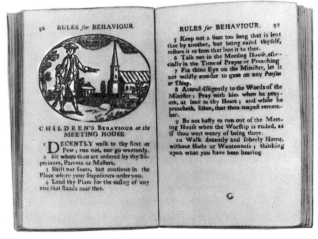

Children were expected to adhere to strict rules during church services and throughout the Sabbath. Unruly behavior was dealt with severely.

Teachers in common schools were poorly paid. Rarely did they receive money; pay was usually meals and a room in which to sleep. Besides teaching, they were expected to perform other duties in the community. Sometimes they even had to dig graves in the town cemetery!

Large towns like Boston had Latin schools. Here students stayed until about the age of fifteen. Latin schools prepared young scholars to be ministers. From the Latin schools they might go on to Harvard College.

Common schools had few teaching aids. There was only the Bible and any books the teacher might own personally. The first real textbook in the colonies did not appear until 1690. That was the famous *New England*

From *Everyday Life: Colonial Times*, published by Good Year Books. © 1997 Walter A. Hazen.

Primer, and it stayed in use for more than a hundred years. In the meantime, students studied the Bible, spelling, reading, writing, and arithmetic. Schools were in session Monday through Saturday, for 9 or 10 hours each day.

Nowhere was school discipline so harsh as in New England. Whippings were everyday occurrences. Sometimes the schoolmaster whipped with what was called a flapper, a leather strap with a hole in the middle. Every blow administered to an unfortunate student raised a blister the size of the hole in the strap.

Sometimes a schoolmaster used a cleft stick to punish a student. The accused was required to go outside and cut a "switch" from a tree. The teacher then cut a cleft, or slit, in the broken-off end of the switch. This was pried open to the desired degree and applied to the nose or tongue of the student. Yes, it pinched! And it might be left in place for hours.

Another favorite form of discipline was the use of whispering sticks. These were wooden gags tied in the mouth with strings, much in the manner of a horse's bit. Whispering sticks were used to discourage talkative students.

Often, the purpose of punishment was to humiliate the student rather than cause physical pain. Bad boys and girls had to wear dunce caps and sit with signs around their necks. The signs ridiculed a particular kind of behavior. A child accused of acting immature might have to wear a sign that read "Baby-Good-for-Nothing." A nail-biter might have to wear one saying "Bite-Finger Baby." A student caught daydreaming might model a sign containing his name preceded by the word "Lazy." Even more humiliating was when a boy and girl caught talking were yoked together like oxen.

Punishment in Dutch schools was less severe. Hands were occasionally spanked, but Dutch parents objected to teachers punishing their children. Thrashings were common in Quaker schools, but there was no attempt to humiliate students as there was in New England.

In the Southern colonies, education never received top priority. The children of plantation owners had private tutors. The wealthier of the planters sent their sons to the best schools in Europe. The girls received just enough education to manage a household. As for the common folk, the wealthy families of the South felt that the commoners' children did not need to be educated, so these children did not have an opportunity to attend school.

This picture, from one of the few remaining copies of the *New England Primer,* shows how students learned to read in colonial times.

Name _____ Date _____

Make a Hornbook

Hornbooks were used in most colonial schools. You can make a hornbook similar to those used by colonial children. The materials will be a little different, but the result will be basically the same.

Here is what you will need:

1. a piece of cardboard (to take the place of wood)

2. two sheets of white typing or printer paper

3. several felt-tip pens or crayons of different colors

4. wax paper or clear food wrap (a substitute for animal horn)

5. glue

6. scissors

Here is how to make it:

1. Cut out a rectangular piece of cardboard 6″ wide and 8″ long.

2. Cut the two sheets of printer paper the same size as the cardboard and glue one piece on either side. Let dry.

3. Cut a handle for your "hornbook" about 7″ long and 2″ wide. Attach the handle with glue to the bottom of one side, allowing for an overlap of about 2″. Let dry.

4. Using a felt-tip pen or crayon, neatly print the alphabet on one side of your hornbook. Print both capital and lower-case letters.

   You might also want to print the numbers 0–9 to one side of the alphabet.

5. On the other side of the hornbook, print the Lord's Prayer or some popular rhyme of the times.

6. Using felt-tip pens or crayons of different colors, decorate the borders of both sides of your hornbook. You may want to draw flowers or birds.

7. Cover both sides of your hornbook with a sheet of wax paper or clear food wrap.

From *Everyday Life: Colonial Times*, published by Good Year Books. © 1997 Walter A. Hazen.

Name _____ Date _____

Write a Lead Paragraph for *The Salem Scoop*

The lead paragraph of a news story should answer the five "W" questions: "Who?" "What?" "When?" "Where?" and "Why?"

There were no newspapers in the early days of colonial America. The first newspaper to appear in 1690 was shut down after one issue. But, for the sake of this activity, let us suppose that newspapers were widespread and that you are a roving reporter for *The Salem Scoop*.

Write the lead paragraph of a story that would go along with the picture on p. 46 and the headline above right. Be sure to include answers to the five "W" questions when you write your paragraph.

The Salem Scoop
★ ★ ★ ★ ★ November 26, 1659 ★ ★ ★ ★ ★

Miles Seymour Placed in Stocks
Second Time Around for Local Man

From *Everyday Life: Colonial Times*, published by Good Year Books. © 1997 Walter A. Hazen.

Name _____ Date _____

What Do You Think About Ducking?

The device shown in the drawing is a ducking stool. It was used in England to punish women accused of gossip and nagging. When the first settlers came to America, they brought the idea of the ducking stool with them.

With a crowd of onlookers gathered around, a woman was tied to a chair attached to a long pole or beam. The pole worked on a pivot or a post at the edge of a stream of water. By pushing up and down on the pole, the officers charged with carrying out the punishment could duck the woman in the water the number of times ordered by the court. Ducking stools were more common in the Northern colonies. They were used in some places as late as the early 1800s.

With these facts in mind, write your opinions to the questions. Continue on a separate sheet of paper if necessary.

1. Do you think women—or anyone, for that matter—should have been punished for gossiping and for "nagging" their spouses? Why or why not? _____

_____

_____

2. The ducking stool was intended more to humiliate than to hurt a person. Were the colonists justified in using it? Why or why not? _____

_____

_____

3. The Bill of Rights to our Constitution prohibits the use of cruel or unusual punishments. In your opinion, was the use of the ducking stool cruel or unusual? Why or why not?

_____

_____

From *Everyday Life: Colonial Times*, published by Good Year Books. © 1997 Walter A. Hazen.

Name _____ Date _____

Solve Some Dame School Math

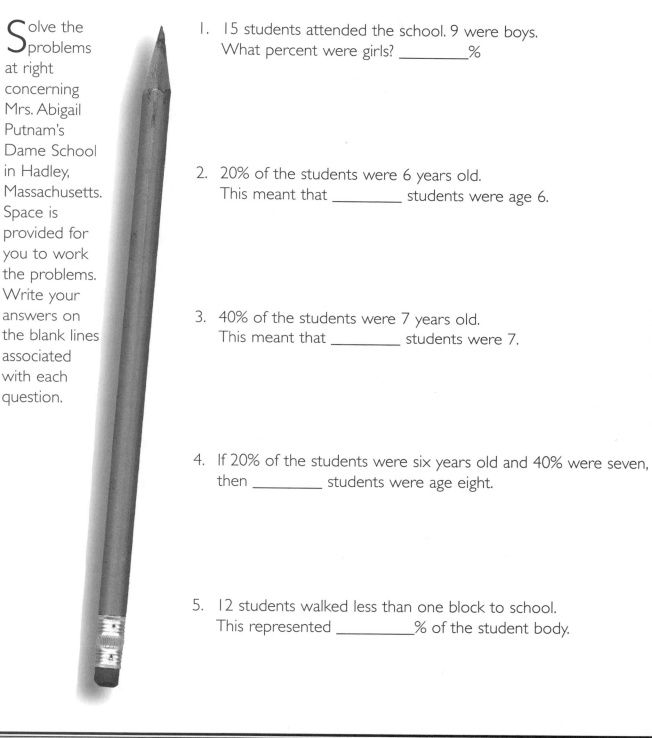

Solve the problems at right concerning Mrs. Abigail Putnam's Dame School in Hadley, Massachusetts. Space is provided for you to work the problems. Write your answers on the blank lines associated with each question.

1. 15 students attended the school. 9 were boys. What percent were girls? _____%

2. 20% of the students were 6 years old. This meant that _____ students were age 6.

3. 40% of the students were 7 years old. This meant that _____ students were 7.

4. If 20% of the students were six years old and 40% were seven, then _____ students were age eight.

5. 12 students walked less than one block to school. This represented _____% of the student body.

From Everyday Life: Colonial Times, published by Good Year Books. © 1997 Walter A. Hazen.

CHAPTER 7

Classes and Occupations

Although America gave people far more freedom than they had experienced in Europe, it did not guarantee them equality. People were not equal from the start. Some settlers arrived rich and grew richer. Others were fortunate and acquired wealth after their arrival. Most colonists belonged to the middle class, while many others arrived poor and stayed that way. Below the poor class of farmers were Native Americans forced to become servants and thousands of blacks brought in from Africa as slaves. And then there were countless indentured servants.

A TOBACCO PLANTATION

Indentured servants were people who sold their labor to others for a prescribed number of years. They were immigrants who did not have the money to pay for passage to America. In return for other people paying their way, they signed contracts to work off the debt once they arrived in America. Most contracts were for three to five years, but a few were for ten. Often entire families became indentured this way. If a father died aboard ship en route to the colonies, his wife and children were obligated to work off the debt. Indentured servants were no better off than slaves, except for one major difference: after their time of servitude was over, they were free to do as they pleased. Some became wealthy landowners themselves.

Not all indentured servants acquired their status in the way described above. Some were children from orphanages who were sent to America to work on farms and in households. This was a common practice among the Dutch. These children also had a set number of years in which they had to donate their labor. When their time was up, they too became free.

Not so for the hundreds of thousands of slaves imported from Africa. Although the Northern colonies abolished slavery in the late 1700s and a few Southern planters freed their laborers, most Africans remained slaves from birth to death. Some were treated kindly, while others endured unspeakable

Slaves on an early Virginia tobacco plantation fill large barrels with tobacco leaves. The man sitting at the left is probably the overseer of the plantation.

From *Everyday Life: Colonial Times*, published by Good Year Books. © 1997 Walter A. Hazen.

hardships and cruelties. Many times, slave parents and children were sold to separate buyers, never to see each other again. Such heartbreaking scenes occurred often at slave markets throughout the South.

There was never a noble class in colonial America. One's position in the world was determined by income and political influence. Through hard work, ability, and a little luck, many had a chance to move up the social ladder.

There was, however, an aristocracy, or upper class. In the South, it consisted of the large plantation owners. These growers of tobacco, rice, indigo, and, later, cotton controlled the political and social affairs of the South throughout the colonial period. In New Netherlands (New York) and New Jersey, large Dutch landowners called patroons were in authority. In New England, wealthy merchants and church leaders made up the aristocracy.

A colonial spinster makes wool yarn at a spinning wheel, a common device in many New England homes.

In the early days of the colonies, people were self-supporting. With the possible exception of salt, everything they needed they made themselves. They built their own houses, made their own clothes and tools, and secured their own food. Only after towns began to grow and prosper did various crafts and occupations become important.

While some colonists preferred life in a town or city, most Americans remained farmers. Farm families took great pride in their freedom and self-sufficiency. Besides, cities were dirty and dangerous. Sanitation facilities were poor and often did not exist at all. Garbage and trash were thrown into the streets. All manner of animals roamed freely, eating the garbage and adding to the problem. Crime and disease were ever present. And there was the constant threat of fire. Since early houses were made of wood and had wooden chimneys, fire could break out at anytime.

Only in the South did one find plantations with huge tracts of land. Rocky soil and severe weather kept farms in New England small. The average farmer there owned a small piece of land on which he grew wheat, corn, and hay. He usually had a cow, some sheep, and a few pigs. His wife tended a small vegetable garden at the back of the house. All work was done without the aid of any advanced implements. For many years, all the farmer had with which to break the soil were a hoe and spade. Later he was able to add a plow. He cut his wheat with a sickle or scythe and threshed it—that is, separated the grain or seeds—with a flail, a special kind of club.

From *Everyday Life: Colonial Times*, published by Good Year Books. © 1997 Walter A. Hazen.

Southern planters set aside parts of their land to grow food for their families and slaves. The rest they planted in one cash crop. In Virginia, Maryland, and parts of North Carolina, the cash crop was tobacco. In South Carolina the cash crops were rice and indigo. Cotton did not become an important crop until after the American Revolution.

Sometimes the wealthy Southern planter did not live on his lands. He kept a house in town and hired an overseer to manage the plantation. An overseer resembled a foreman on a western ranch. It was his responsibility to supervise the planting and harvesting of the crop. He gave daily orders to the slaves and saw that everything on the plantation ran smoothly.

In the North, some colonists made fortunes as merchants. Shipbuilding became a leading industry. So did fishing. Codfish caught off the coast of New England was dried and salted and shipped to Europe. Whaling was another important industry. Whale oil was used in lamps, and whalebones provided the stays for women's dresses and corsets.

As towns grew, so did the demand for skilled craftsmen. Anyone who mastered a trade could earn a living in the colonies. Sometimes towns even advertised when they needed a craftsman in a certain area.

A cobbler hard at work. Since colonial people walked everywhere they went and wore shoes out quickly, the cobbler was a busy craftsman.

Every town had its blacksmith. He not only made horseshoes and oxshoes, but locks, hinges, tools, nails, and plows as well. A town might also have a whitesmith, usually referred to as a tinsmith. A whitesmith made and repaired items made of tin. Another craftsman who worked with metals was a pewterer. A pewterer made plates and other utensils from pewter, a mixture of copper, tin, and lead.

The cobbler who made and repaired shoes was much in demand. Because people walked almost everywhere they went, shoes wore out quickly. Round-trip walks from farm to town of over twenty miles were not unusual. The colonial shoemaker was unique in that he did not make "pairs" of shoes. There was not a shoe for the left foot and another for the right. Both shoes were made the same and could be worn on either foot.

At first there was little work for tailors and joiners, or cabinetmakers. Early colonists made all their clothes and furniture themselves. But as people

From *Everyday Life: Colonial Times*, published by Good Year Books. © 1997 Walter A. Hazen.

prospered, they had more need for craftsmen who could mend clothes or make furniture. Tailors stayed busy altering hand-me-down clothing for children. Cabinetmakers turned out beautiful chairs, tables, and other fine furniture.

Among other craftsmen were watchmakers, hatters, gunsmiths, bakers, and coopers. Coopers made barrels, and their products were in constant demand. Everything that was exported from the colonies was shipped in barrels. This included rice, flour, beef, and fish. Especially large barrels called hogsheads were needed to ship tobacco. The tobacco was packed in these hogsheads and rolled to wharves, where ships waited to take the profitable commodity to Europe.

Once the colonies were well established, craftsmen with building skills had all the work they wanted. Thousands of carpenters built houses, barns, fences, churches, and other structures of wood. Bricklayers, masons, and painters also found plenty to do. None of these artisans suffered for work while people continued to pour into the colonies.

Carpenters at work in early Plymouth. As more people came to the colonies, the demand for carpenters' services rose. From an old copper engraving.

There were no schools in colonial times that taught any trade or craft. A young man wanting to learn a skill became an apprentice to a skilled craftsman. This was true even in the law profession, where many colonial lawyers acquired their legal knowledge while studying under a seasoned lawyer.

In most cases, parents made an agreement with a craftsman to take on their son as an apprentice. The craftsman fed, clothed, and housed the boy for an apprenticeship that usually lasted for six or seven years. After that time, the young man was qualified to strike out on his own. This method of learning a trade was similar to the craft guilds of medieval Europe. Even such famous Americans as Benjamin Franklin began their careers as apprentices. Franklin was apprenticed to his brother as a teenager to learn the printing trade.

From Everyday Life: Colonial Times, *published by Good Year Books. © 1997 Walter A. Hazen.*

Name _____ Date _____

Finish a Letter to a Friend in Salem

Pretend you are a young boy or young girl living in Salem, Massachusetts, in colonial times. You and your family have come to Charleston, South Carolina, to visit relatives. One day, while walking through the streets of Charleston with your father, you pass a slave market where slaves are being sold. You are shocked by what you see.

Finish the following letter to a friend in Salem. The first two sentences are done for you.

Date _____

Dear _____,

    Today Father and I came upon a slave auction in town. It was the most heartbreaking thing I have ever seen.

_____

_____

_____

_____

_____

_____

_____

_____

_____

_____

_____

_____

_____

_____

_____

Your friend,

_____

From *Everyday Life: Colonial Times*, published by Good Year Books. © 1997 Walter A. Hazen.

Name _____ Date _____

Name That Craftsman

As the colonies grew, so did the number of skilled craftsmen offering their services.

At right are ten types of craftsmen who were important in colonial times. Some were discussed in the chapter. You may need a dictionary to identify the others.

Select the correct craftsman from the word box and write the word on the blank line in front of each statement.

cooper	blacksmith
whitesmith	tinker
tailor	potter
cobbler	cabinetmaker
sawyer	chandler

1. _____ "I make barrels."

2. _____ "Among other things, I make hinges and locks."

3. _____ "I make things of tin. Sometimes I am called a tinsmith."

4. _____ "I am also called a shoemaker."

5. _____ "I alter and mend clothes."

6. _____ "I was at first called a joiner because I join pieces of wood together to make furniture."

7. _____ "I cut down trees and turn them into lumber."

8. _____ "I make candles."

9. _____ "I make and repair pots and pans."

10. _____ "I make earthenware dishes and other utensils."

From *Everyday Life: Colonial Times*, published by Good Year Books. © 1997 Walter A. Hazen.

Name _____ Date _____

Find the Main Idea

Most paragraphs contain one central or main idea. How good are you at picking these out?

Refer to the Chapter 7 narrative text you just read. On the lines following the paragraph numbers at right, write what you consider to be the main idea expressed in each.

Paragraph 1

_____

_____

_____

Paragraph 3

_____

_____

_____

Paragraph 5

_____

_____

_____

Paragraph 9

_____

_____

_____

Paragraph 11

_____

_____

_____

Paragraph 19

_____

_____

_____

From *Everyday Life: Colonial Times*, published by Good Year Books. © 1997 Walter A. Hazen.

Name _____ Date _____

Roll Out the Barrel

You learned in Chapter 7 that most products in colonial times were shipped in barrels and that the cooper's handiwork was always in demand.

At the right are several problems dealing with barrel capacity. Use the table below to solve them.

I gallon	=	4 quarts
I quart	=	2 pints
I barrel	=	31.5 gallons
I barrel	=	3.28 bushels
I hogshead	=	2 barrels

1. The Boar's Inn in colonial Williamsburg ordered four barrels of ale from a brewer.

    One barrel was equal to _____ quarts of ale.

    All four barrels contained _____ quarts of ale.

    Three quarts of ale were equal to _____ pints.

2. If 500 pounds of tobacco could be shipped in one hogshead, how many hogsheads would it take to ship 3,000 pounds? How many barrels would it take?

    _____ hogsheads

    _____ barrels

3. Twelve barrels of rice were shipped from a South Carolina plantation to a port in England. How many bushels of rice did the barrels contain?

    _____ bushels

Name _____ Date _____

Compare Cities Then and Now

Go back and read paragraph 8 of Chapter 7 again. Then answer the questions at right.

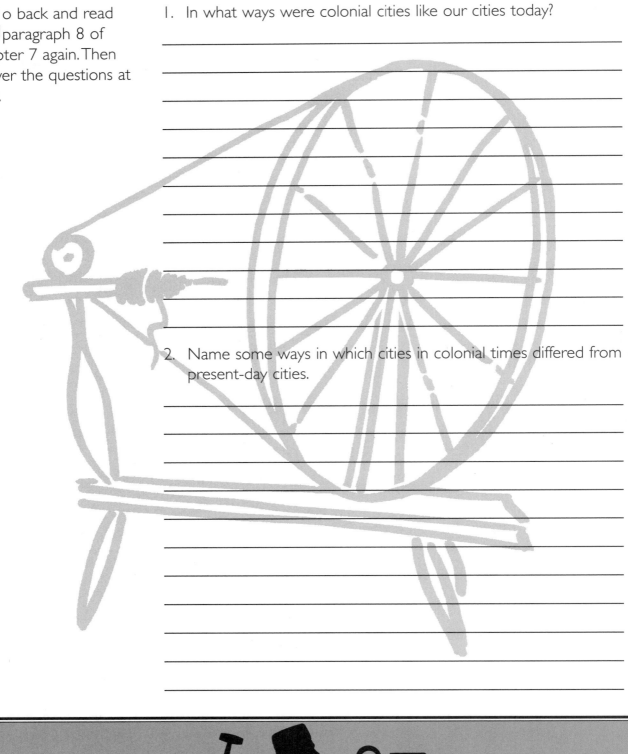

1. In what ways were colonial cities like our cities today?

_____

_____

_____

_____

_____

_____

_____

_____

_____

_____

_____

_____

2. Name some ways in which cities in colonial times differed from present-day cities.

_____

_____

_____

_____

_____

_____

_____

_____

_____

_____

Travel and Communication

In the early days of America, it was often easier to travel to England than to make a journey from one colony to another.

Roads did not exist. What passed for trails were simply Indian footpaths through the forests. Those colonists who dared to travel them faced uncertainty and constant danger. Often they became lost.

The usual method of travel was by water. Most settlements were built near the ocean or by a river or stream, making travel by boat the easiest way to get around. From the American Indians, the colonists learned to make birch-bark canoes and dugouts. A canoe would hold only one or two occupants, but a dugout could accommodate six people. Dugouts were made from hollowed-out pine and measured about 20 feet long and 2 or 3 feet wide. It oftentimes took three weeks to make a dugout.

As early as 1631, a ferry service began in Massachusetts. The first ferries were canoes in which the rower took a passenger across a river for a few pennies. The passenger's horse swam along behind the canoe. There was no charge to "ferry" the horse across.

In time, walking as a means of getting someplace gave way to horseback. Indian footpaths became wider, and more people began to travel. Because there were not enough horses to go around, a unique system of travel called ride-and-tie was used. Four people might set out on a journey together. Two walked ahead, while two rode on a horse—one sitting in the saddle and the other on a cushion called a pillion. The two on horseback caught up with and passed the two who had left on foot. After riding for perhaps a mile, they dismounted and tied the horse to a tree. They then set out on foot themselves. The two who had walked ahead earlier would eventually arrive at the tree, take the horse, and ride on for a mile. Then they too would dismount and tie the horse to a tree. The two original riders would complete

Traveling by canoe was the easiest way to get around in the early days of America. Colonists learned from the Indians how to make swift canoes.

From *Everyday Life: Colonial Times*, published by Good Year Books. © 1997 Walter A. Hazen.

A sloop sails the Hudson River. Sloops carried supplies and passengers up rivers and along the coast.

their walking portion, take the horse again, and ride on for another mile before again leaving it at a tree. This alternating of riding and walking continued until the four reached their destination.

The first roads built in the colonies were called mast roads. They were laid out for the sole purpose of transporting trees that were used for masts on British ships. Most began deep in the forest and went straight to the sea. They were of little value to a traveler, who usually desired to go to a place in a different direction.

Township roads were little better. Because they ran through private lands, each farmer could route them as he pleased. A road might run straight for a while, then veer around a corn field or wheat field or some other part of a farm. The farmer could also place a gate any place he chose. This made it necessary for the traveler to stop, open the gate, walk his horse or cart through, and close the gate behind him before moving on.

It is not surprising that most people chose to travel by boat. Vessels called sloops traveled up and down the rivers and along the coast of the Atlantic Ocean. If the weather was good, a sloop could travel between New York and Philadelphia in about three days. In the South, plantations were so scattered and isolated that the only way of reaching some of them was by water. Planters went to town, to church, and to visit friends by boat.

In time, roads improved and the stagecoach became another means of transportation. A few wealthy merchants and planters owned coaches in the seventeenth century, but coaches did not come into wide use until the early 1700s.

Travel by stagecoach was uncomfortable, to say the least. The traveler was jolted and bounced around when roads became rutted by heavy rains. Sometimes the coach got stuck in mud and all the passengers had to get out and help push it free. At other times, passengers were asked to "lean to the right" or "lean to the left" to prevent a coach from overturning on the washed-out, uneven roads. Stagecoaches were cold and damp in winter and hot and dusty in summer. A trip from New York to Philadelphia took two

From *Everyday Life: Colonial Times*, published by Good Year Books. © 1997 Walter A. Hazen.

days, while one from New York to Boston required about a week. At intervals along the way, weary travelers could rest their jarred bodies and acquire a meal at inns that had begun to spring up along the routes.

Inns in colonial America were known by various names. Besides inns, they were called taverns, ordinaries, and victuallings. Individual inns had such quaint names as The Old Swan, the Red Horse Tavern, and the Plow and Harrow. For a few shillings, a traveler got a room, several meals, and a quantity of wine and beer. Women usually preferred to take their meals privately in their own rooms, not desiring to join the sometimes boisterous crowd at the bar.

Inns also served as social clubs for local residents. Men would gather, drink beer, and catch up on the latest news. Upper-class gentlemen played cards or backgammon. Commoners entertained themselves with checkers, skittles, and shuffleboard. Since much drinking took place during these games, most colonies passed laws limiting the hours an inn could stay open and the amount of liquor it could sell.

Inns served still another purpose. They were, in effect, America's first post offices. The post, or person who brought mail once a month, left all the mail for that town at a local inn. Letters were spread out on a table for all to see and check. Anyone finding his or her name on a letter claimed it and paid the postage. Postage in those days was high, and it was always paid by the receiver of the letter.

Before a regular postal service was established, letters were entrusted to any traveler going to the same destination as the letter. In colonial times, letters were not placed in envelopes. They were simply folded in half and sealed with melted wax. Writers had their own seals that they stamped into the wax to identify the sender.

As roads improved, the stagecoach became an important means of travel in colonial America. Inns along the way provided much-needed rest stops for weary travelers.

From *Everyday Life: Colonial Times*, published by Good Year Books. © 1997 Walter A. Hazen.

A letter carrier around 1740 signals his approach, perhaps to a wayside inn where letters were left for recipients to claim.

Even when letters started being delivered to individual residences, house and street addresses were not in general use. The sender often included directions on the letter to aid the postman in finding the proper place. A typical address might read as follows:

Mr. Thomas Crawford
3rd House Past the
Sharkshead Inn
Hadley, Massachusetts

Mail was delivered in a variety of ways. Some post carriers walked. In winter, when rivers and streams froze, they skated across to their destination. Others made their rounds on horseback. Sometimes, to relieve boredom, those on horseback knitted socks while sitting in their saddle. In time, post offices were established throughout the colonies and mail coaches came into use.

Like post offices, newspapers came late to the colonies. The reason was a shortage of paper. Also, printing presses and ink had to be brought over from England. Newspapers did not become widespread in America until the early part of the eighteenth century.

A town crier bellows out the news for the benefit of the local townspeople. Town criers were important in the days before newspapers.

But colonists were not without news. Every village and most towns had a town crier. This was an official who went around ringing a bell or beating a drum and relaying the latest news to all within earshot. Towns also had a watchman. A watchman walked the streets at night, making certain everyone was safe from fire and other dangers. The watchman also provided up-to-date weather reports for people lying in their beds and not yet asleep. Along with his usual "Twelve o'clock and all's well," he might chant something like "One o'clock and a fair wind blows!" or "Two o'clock and the snow is falling!"

From *Everyday Life: Colonial Times*, published by Good Year Books. © 1997 Walter A. Hazen.

Name _____ Date _____

Solve Some Math Traveling Problems

You have learned that travel in colonial times was very slow. You will remember that it took a stagecoach two days to travel from Philadelphia to New York and a full week to go from New York to Boston.

With these facts in mind, solve the problems at right. Space is provided for you to work each problem.

1. The distance from Boston to New York is about 208 miles (335k). How many miles or kilometers each day did the stagecoach in colonial times average? (Round off your answer.)

   The stagecoach averaged _____ miles (kilometers) each day.

2. What speed must an automobile today average to cover the distance from Boston to New York in 4 hours? (Round off your answer.)

   An automobile must average _____ miles (kilometers) per hour.

3. A stagecoach in colonial times traveling the 776 miles (1,261k) from New York to Charleston, South Carolina, averaged 32 miles (52k) a day. How many days did it take to make the trip?

   It took _____ days.

Name _____ Date _____

Create a Signboard for an Inn

Inns in colonial times were identified by decorative signboards that swung on posts near their entrances. Great care was taken in the making of these signs. They involved the combined efforts of painters, joiners, and other craftsmen.

In the space provided on this page, create a signboard that might have hung in front of a colonial inn. Remember that inns and taverns bore the names of animals, objects, people—almost anything. Look through a book or encyclopedia for ideas.

Make your signboard as decorative and as colorful as possible.

From *Everyday Life: Colonial Times,* published by Good Year Books. © 1997 Walter A. Hazen.

Name _____ Date _____

Keep a Stagecoach Diary

Imagine yourself living in colonial times and making the two-day trip by stagecoach from New York to Philadelphia.

Make up diary entries for the two days. Think of occurrences that could have taken place on such a journey.

April 12, 1752

Dear Diary,

_____
_____
_____
_____
_____
_____
_____
_____
_____
_____
_____
_____
_____
_____
_____
_____
_____
_____
_____

April 13, 1752

Dear Diary,

_____
_____
_____
_____
_____
_____
_____
_____
_____
_____
_____
_____
_____
_____
_____
_____
_____
_____

Name _____ Date _____

Compare and Contrast Two Eras

You have learned that travel and communication in colonial America were primitive compared to the way they are in America today. On the chart at right, compare colonial times with today in regards to the four items listed in the left-hand column.

	Colonial Times	Today
Travel		
Lodging		
Postal Service		
Communication		

From *Everyday Life: Colonial Times*, published by Good Year Books. © 1997 Walter A. Hazen.

CHAPTER 9

Health and Medicine

"Tie a white herring to the sole of each foot and call me in the morning."

This might have been the advice given to a patient by a colonial doctor if telephones had existed in those days. Tying fish to the soles of the feet was a common prescription for fever in colonial times!

Some mention was made of disease and treatments in Chapter 1. But a closer look at the ways in which colonists attempted to cope with illness is both interesting and worthwhile.

A herring tied to the sole of each foot was a certain cure for fever, or so thought the people of colonial times. Can you think of any folk remedies today that are just as far-fetched?

You have learned that few doctors were available in colonial times. Those who called themselves physicians usually had little knowledge of health and medicine. The first medical school in America did not even open until 1765. Consequently, people were more likely to rely on home remedies than put their trust in a local doctor.

Life expectancy in seventeenth-century America was short. This was due in part to the high rate of infant deaths from epidemics that swept the colonies. It was also the result of the large number of women who died either in childbirth or as the result of having too many children. It was not uncommon for women to die in their thirties. With life expectancy in America today at about 75 years, it is hard to visualize the average colonist living only to the age of 35.

Medical knowledge in early America was almost nonexistent. Ignorance of germs and sanitation caused disease to spread and made for terrible epidemics. No one knew to quarantine patients with contagious diseases like smallpox and diphtheria. No one understood that dirty clothing and bed linens were breeding grounds for vermin and bacteria. No one knew to boil water to make it safe for drinking. Everyone threw garbage in the streets and let human waste pollute their wells. People ate too much and consumed too much alcohol, both leading to many deaths from strokes and heart attacks.

From *Everyday Life: Colonial Times*, published by Good Year Books. © 1997 Walter A. Hazen.

Doctors were just as limited in their knowledge of disease as were common people. They knew nothing about antiseptics or hygiene. Operations were performed every day by doctors who neither washed their hands nor sterilized their instruments. When a doctor was not available, surgical procedures such as amputations were performed by blacksmiths. And the latter, like the doctors, did not know to wash their hands or to boil their saw in hot water before proceeding.

Coupled with ignorance was superstition. Most colonists believed disease was associated with God or the supernatural. They believed God punished those who did not obey his laws; witches put spells on people and made them sick; constellations and voodoo caused people to sicken and die. Superstition was even connected with cures. Some people thought the king's touch could cure

Women at work finding leeches. Leeches were used to bleed patients in the hopes that such practice would release the bad vapors that caused illness. From a colored engraving.

epilepsy and scrofula, a form of tuberculosis.

Death from diseases that are curable today spared no one. Rich and poor alike died from typhoid, yellow fever, malaria, measles, smallpox, pneumonia, and typhoid. And conditions were not much better even at the end of the colonial period.

A case in point concerns the death of George Washington. The retired President had gone for a horse ride on his estate at Mount Vernon on a cold, wet December day in 1799. He later contracted what was at first believed to be a severe cold. Matters quickly grew worse, and it was clear that Washington was gravely ill. Three doctors were summoned. Had they possessed any real medical knowledge at all, they probably could have saved Washington's life. As it was, they relied on the same techniques used by doctors from the early days of the colonies. First, they performed phlebotomy, the practice of bleeding a patient. It was thought that many diseases were caused either by "bad vapors" or by too much pressure in the veins—hence the belief in bleeding a patient. But Washington's three doctors got a little carried away in the bleeding

From *Everyday Life: Colonial Times*, published by Good Year Books. © 1997 Walter A. Hazen.

process. They bled their patient for several days, during which time he lost half the blood in his body. They also gave him a very powerful cathartic, or laxative, to clean the bowels. Hoping to remove the "bad vapors" from his body, they applied a mixture of ground beetles to his throat. This caused blisters that were thought to help draw out the vapors. It is no surprise that Washington died shortly afterwards, having shown no improvement whatsoever from the "treatment" he received from the three distinguished doctors.

Phlebotomy was the standard treatment for many illnesses, and was performed with a nonsterile instrument called a fleam. Phlebotomy was prescribed for fever, pneumonia, malaria, and upset stomach. When it was thought necessary to bleed a part of the body where an incision was unwise (such as around the eyes or mouth), a leech was used. Doctors kept leeches in jars on shelves in their offices. So did barbers and blacksmiths, who often doubled as surgeons.

Doctors, as well as barbers and blacksmiths who sometimes performed medical services, kept jars of leeches on hand with which to bleed patients. From an old woodcut.

Mixtures designed to make patients vomit or empty their bowels were also standard treatments. Often these "medicines" did more harm than good. Weakness and dehydration may have caused as many deaths as the illnesses being treated.

It is not surprising that many people chose to treat themselves. All manner of home remedies appeared. If bleeding did not bring down a fever, then roasted and powdered frogs would certainly do the trick! If the fever was accompanied by chills, a bath in a liquid mixed with hot human urine was said to bring relief. Swollen glands? It was believed these could be reduced to normal size by drinking white wine with a prescribed number of wood lice mixed in. And if you had just been bitten by a rabid animal? No problem. Eating onions in large amounts would surely ward off rabies!

Even distinguished colonists got into the act of concocting home remedies. John Winthrop, Jr., the governor of Connecticut, boasted of a private cure-all made from wine-vinegar with a liberal amount of powdered crab eyes stirred in!

But not all home remedies and doctors' prescriptions were completely useless. Some could actually help ease the symptoms of a particular disease. An example is Dr. Zorobbabel Endicott's remedy for a chill. The Salem, Massachusetts, physician recommended several bowls of hot turtle broth to warm a quivering patient. Like chicken soup, it was probably effective in certain cases.

Here's a treatment for illness in colonial times that is still around today: this feverish man is sipping hot broth. However, his is probably made from turtle instead of chicken.

Surgery was performed as little as possible in colonial times. Doctors had limited knowledge of the body and no way of seeing what went on inside of it. But sometimes it was necessary to amputate a limb or set a broken bone. The only anesthetics available were opium and rum, and patients were made as groggy as possible with one of these. If the surgeon did not have access to either pain killer, the patient had to grit his or her teeth and bear it. A stick or bullet was placed in the patient's mouth to bite down on and make the pain a little more tolerable.

Dentistry was just as painful. Since there were no dentists in those days, teeth were usually pulled by barbers and blacksmiths. Sometimes, in rural areas, the task fell to the strongest man around at the time. A knife was used to cut the gum away from the tooth, and it was pulled out with a pair of pliers. Tooth extraction was a commonplace occurrence in colonial times. No one had any idea that tooth decay could be prevented. A tooth was allowed to decay to the point where the pain was unbearable. Only then did the sufferer consent to having it pulled out. It is not surprising that most colonists lost all of their teeth by the age of thirty.

The colonial period was almost over before any advancements in health and medicine were made. The first hospital in America—Pennsylvania Hospital—was built in Philadelphia in 1751. Fourteen years later, the first medical school opened its doors at the University of Pennsylvania. Ever so slowly, improvements in the understanding and treatment of disease became a reality. By the time of the American Revolution in 1776, there were approximately 3,500 doctors in the colonies. Of this number, 200, or roughly 6 percent, had earned a medical degree. Six percent was certainly an improvement over the zero percent of a few short years before!

From *Everyday Life: Colonial Times*, published by Good Year Books. © 1997 Walter A. Hazen.

Name _____ Date _____

Test Your Medical Vocabulary

Fill in the blanks in the sentences at right using the words below.

○ antibiotics

○ bewitched

○ deaths

○ diseases

○ doctors

○ immunized

○ ingredients

○ medical

○ natural

○ patients

○ prevented

○ quacks

○ sanitation

○ survive

○ young

You will remember that many children in colonial times died _____.
There were few _____ and no _____ schools. Some men who called themselves "doctors" were little better than _____. They gave _____ strange mixtures of herbs and other _____ that often did more harm than good. Any sick person who did not respond to such treatment was said to be _____.

Today, we know that diseases have _____ causes. We have learned that many _____ can be easily _____. Understanding and practicing simple rules of _____ can prevent many of the diseases that plagued the colonists.

When children today start school, they are _____ against infections that colonial children usually did not _____. Such diseases as diphtheria, smallpox, measles, and whooping cough are rare today in the United States. Also, _____ such as penicillin and sulfa have proved beneficial in treating other illnesses that caused the early _____ of many colonial children.

Name _____ Date _____

Write About Going to the "Blacksmith"

In Chapter 9 you learned about the sad state of dentistry in the colonies. It was not surprising that many people found themselves completely toothless in the prime of life. Going to the "dentist" was a terrifying ordeal, and most people put it off as long as possible.

Pretend you are living in colonial times and you have just had your first tooth extracted by a blacksmith. Write a letter to a friend in a neighboring town describing the experience.

Date _____

Dear _____,

_____

_____

_____

_____

_____

_____

_____

_____

_____

_____

_____

_____

_____

_____

_____

_____

_____

_____

Your friend,

_____

From *Everyday Life: Colonial Times*, published by Good Year Books. © 1997 Walter A. Hazen.

Name _____ Date _____

Why Do Some People Live Longer?

The average life expectancy today is about 75 years—40 more years than in colonial times. With these facts in mind, answer the questions at right.

1. Many people in colonial America did live to a ripe old age. Some lived past their 100th year. If this is so, why was the average life expectancy only 35?

_____

_____

_____

_____

_____

2. List any four reasons why you think people today live so much longer than before.

_____

_____

_____

_____

_____

3. With America's population growing older each year, can you think of some problems this poses for our society?

_____

_____

_____

_____

_____

Name _____   Date _____

Solve a Medicine Crossword

Across

1. Surgical instrument used in phlebotomies

3. Bad _____ were said to cause some illnesses.

5. Fish tied to the bottom of the feet was a remedy for this

8. Craftsman who often performed amputations

9. Large amounts of onions were thought to prevent this disease

11. A type of colonial anesthetic

Down

2. Blood sucking worm used to bleed a patient

4. The practice of bleeding a patient

6. Dr. Zorobabbel
   _____

7. His touch was believed to cure scrofula

9. Another colonial pain-killer

10. Live expectancy in colonial times was thirty-
    _____

From *Everyday Life: Colonial Times*, published by Good Year Books. © 1997 Walter A. Hazen.

CHAPTER 10

Relations with the American Indians

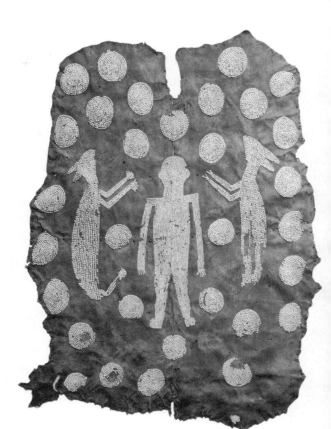

The early colonists and the American Indians who lived along the Atlantic seaboard got along well at first—especially in New England. But whether in New England or Jamestown, the English settlers would have starved to death without the help of the Indians.

As was stated in Chapter 4, the Indians taught the colonists how to grow corn, which became a staple food. In addition, they showed the newcomers how to tap maple trees and boil the sap into maple sugar, as well as how to snare fish and trap wild animals.

However, relations with the Indians around Jamestown were shaky at best. The colony might have perished if not for the leadership of Captain John Smith. Smith maintained an uneasy peace with the Indians by befriending their chief, Powhatan. Powhatan's daughter, Pocahontas, later married one of the Jamestown settlers, John Rolfe, in 1614.

Chief Powhatan's shell-decorated, deerskin robe. The chief was the father of Pocahontas, who is said to have saved the life of John Smith.

Powhatan was succeeded as chief by his brother Opechancanough. Opechancanough hated the "English" (settlers) and planned to drive them back into the ocean. In 1622 he attacked the settlement and killed over 300 of the English. Had he continued the fight, the colony might have been destroyed. But he waited twenty-two years before attacking again in 1644. By that time, Jamestown was firmly established, and, although more than 500 settlers were killed, the Indians were defeated and forced to retreat into the wilderness. Opechancanough himself was captured and shot. Jamestown survived, and there were no major problems with the Indians in Virginia afterwards.

Both the Pilgrims and the Wampanoag Indians who lived around Plymouth held strange ideas about each other. The Wampanoags wondered why the white man had braved such a terrible ocean to come to their shore. Many reasoned it was because he had burned all the firewood in his country and was looking for a new supply. And those English ships! What kind of tree

From Everyday Life: Colonial Times, published by Good Year Books. © 1997 Walter A. Hazen.

was used to make them? Whatever it was, it had to be gigantic, for the Indians believed that each ship was hollowed out from a single tree!

The Pilgrims at first did not believe the Indians to be a different race. They thought Indians had white skin that had turned bronze from the sun and all the dye they applied to their bodies. Some even believed the Indians were actually Jews who were descendants of the ten lost tribes of Israel.

At first, the Pilgrims did not see American Indians as hostile or threatening. Instead, they viewed them as curiosities and as possible converts to Christianity. Although relations were good from the start, a number of things about the Indians irked the Plymouth settlers. Not only did many of them enjoy drinking and gambling a little too much, but the Indians' manner of dress bothered the Pilgrim fathers. As stated in Chapter 3, the Pilgrims covered their bodies from head to toe, with very little skin showing. The Indians, on the other hand, wore loincloths in both summer and winter. Furthermore, the men greased their bodies with animal fat or fish oil to help keep them warm in winter and keep the mosquitoes from biting them in summer. It didn't bother them in the least that their appearance irritated the Pilgrims. In fact, there were manners of the Pilgrims that bothered the Indians. For example, they thought beards worn by the English were repulsive.

Despite their differences, the Pilgrims and the Wampanoags got along well. Massasoit, the head Wampanoag chief, remained a true friend to the Pilgrims throughout his life. So did lesser chiefs like Squanto and Samoset. All three had experienced early contact with the English. Squanto and Samoset spoke English quite well.

The Pilgrims, along with their Wampanoag Indian friends, celebrate a bountiful harvest in 1607. What was America's first Thanksgiving celebration lasted for three days.

From *Everyday Life: Colonial Times*, published by Good Year Books. © 1997 Walter A. Hazen.

With the help of Squanto and others, the Plymouth colony survived the first harsh winter. Spring arrived and crops were planted. Then came fall and a bountiful harvest. The Pilgrims had an abundant supply of corn and wheat, as well as deer, wild turkeys, and seafood. They decided to celebrate and thank God for their good fortune. Chief Massasoit and ninety of his men were invited to a feast. The Indians themselves brought five deer to add to the already huge amount of food. This was the first Thanksgiving, and the celebration lasted for three days. Games were played, and the Wampanoags and Pilgrims hunted together. The Indians left as friends and remained so for the next fifty years.

Not all the Indians of New England were as friendly. The Pequots of Connecticut felt squeezed between the English to the north and the Dutch moving up from the south. In 1637 they fought a brief war to drive out the Europeans. They failed, and the entire Pequot tribe was destroyed.

To protect themselves against Indian attacks, the colonists built blockhouses. A blockhouse was a two-story fort built of logs. Holes were cut in the walls through which muskets could be fired at attackers. Blockhouses saved many lives during Indian and colonist confrontations, offering refuge to people from nearby settlements and farms. Colonists who did not live in the vicinity of a blockhouse managed as best they could. Many houses had secret closets in which women and children hid during Indian attacks.

In 1660, Chief Massasoit of the Wampanoags died. He was succeeded by his son Metacomet, whom the English called King Philip. For several years, Philip honored the treaty his father had made with the Pilgrims. But he knew that war with the white man was inevitable. As each year passed, the colonists grabbed more and more of the Indians' land. Soon there would be no land left on which they could hunt or fish.

What was called King Philip's War broke out in 1675. Many of the New England tribes united under Philip to wipe out the Europeans. It was a very bloody war. Both sides committed terrible atrocities against men, women, and children. No fewer than twelve towns were destroyed and 2,000 colonists killed. Indian losses were much greater. King Philip himself was shot and killed and his wife and son were sold into slavery in the West Indies.

In times of confrontation with the Indians, early colonists withdrew inside of blockhouses for protection. Blockhouses were located near the centers of settlements to enable everyone to reach them quickly.

But American Indian losses could not be measured in lives and property alone. The Indians lost something far more important: freedom. Although occasional attacks and massacres continued throughout the colonial period, never again would the Indians roam free throughout the New England wilderness.

Sometimes students of history fall into the habit of calling attacks by Indians "massacres" and those by whites "wars." Such labels are unfair to American Indians and do not tell the true story. To be sure, Indians were guilty of horrible massacres; but so were the colonists. Often, atrocities committed by one side led the other to seek revenge in a like manner. Sometimes massacres resulted from a single act of violence on the part of a lone Indian or white settler. At other times, a simple insult might be enough to spark an uprising or a war.

Relations between Indians and colonists were much better in other parts of the colonies. In Pennsylvania and Rhode Island, there were few problems between the races. Settlers in those colonies treated the Indians well and paid them a fair price for their land. It is said that not a single Quaker was killed in Pennsylvania during the lifetime of William Penn, who founded the colony. In Maryland, no problems arose, because the English who settled there chose land that the Indians had given up as unfit for habitation.

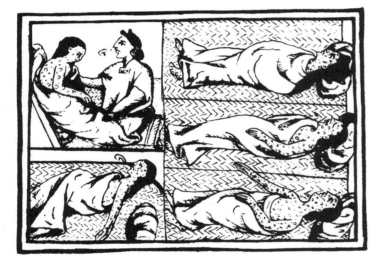

Diseases introduced by white settlers decimated the Indian population of America. Entire tribes were virtually wiped out by smallpox.

Many American Indians paid a high price for their friendly contact with the settlers—their lives. The settlers exposed the Indians to diseases such as smallpox and measles that they had no natural immunity to. Some estimates are that within the first 100 years, 90 percent of the American Indian population died as a result of contact with the settlers.

In summary, problems between the Indians and colonists resulted from cultural differences and the settlers' hunger for land. It was only when the Indians felt threatened that they grew hostile. They saw their territory dwindling, their people being killed by European diseases, and their whole way of life in jeopardy. Matters finally reached the point where they had to fight to protect their very existence.

From *Everyday Life: Colonial Times*, published by Good Year Books. © 1997 Walter A. Hazen.

Name _____ Date _____

Suppose History Had Been Different

In an effort to protect their very existence, the American Indians tried to wipe out the English settlements along the Atlantic seaboard in the late 1600s. They failed, obviously, and the colonies survived and prospered.

But suppose things had turned out differently. Suppose the Indians had succeeded in driving the white man from America's shores. And suppose that Europeans had given up on the idea of colonizing America and never returned for another try.

With these thoughts in mind, how do you think our country's history might have been different? What would America be like today?

Write your thoughts on the lines at right.

Name _____ Date _____

Interpret a Bar Graph

From *Everyday Life: Colonial Times,* published by Good Year Books. © 1997 Walter A. Hazen.

It is estimated that between 850,000 and 1,000,000 Indians lived in what is now the United States at the time the Jamestown and Massachusetts colonies were founded. Some 9,000 lived in what later became Virginia. About 16,000 lived in the New England area.

The graph on this page compares the Indian populations of Virginia and New England with Indian groups in three other places.

Use the graph to answer the questions at right.

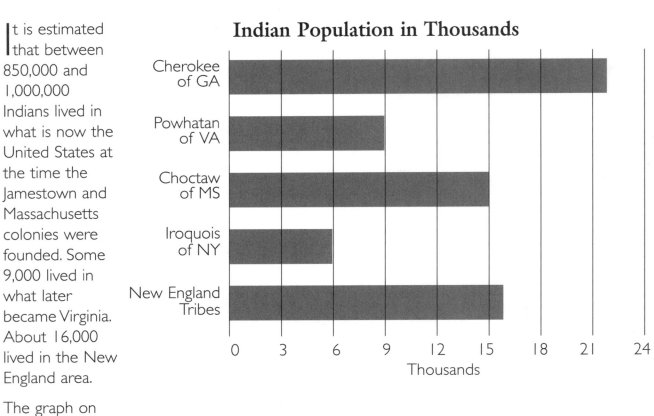

Indian Population in Thousands

Cherokee of GA
Powhatan of VA
Choctaw of MS
Iroquois of NY
New England Tribes

0   3   6   9   12   15   18   21   24

Thousands

1. What is the total Indian population represented on the graph?
    _____

2. What percent of the total Indian population did the New England tribes make up?

    _____%

3. How many more Cherokee were there than Choctaw?
    _____

4. What was the combined Indian population of Georgia and Mississippi?
    _____

5. What percent of the total Indian population did the Powhatan make up? _____%

Name _____ Date _____

Dramatize a Historical Event

Divide the class into four groups. Each group should choose one of the skits at right. Use your imagination and creative skills in planning your skit. Each skit should be about five minutes in length.

Any student in your group not participating directly in a skit could help make simple props or critique the skits and rate them at the conclusion of the activity.

There is a lead-in to each skit to help you in your planning.

SKIT 1—Indians Showing the Pilgrims How to Plant Corn

You know by now the story of how Squanto and other Indians taught the Pilgrims how to grow corn.

Squanto, of course, could speak English. But suppose he had not been able to. Plan to use gestures and sign language in this skit.

SKIT 2—Indians Buying Cloth from Pilgrims

New England Indians used bead money called wampum. Wampum was made from various kinds and colors of seashells. The Indians strung the shells on animal gut or hemp and then wove the strands into either belts or wrist and waist bands. A single strand of wampum was worth about 7 or 8 shillings in English money.

Center this skit around the question: How much wampum would a group of Indians need in order to buy a prescribed amount of woolen cloth from a Pilgrim?

SKIT 3—Pocahontas Saving John Smith's Life

Before Pocahontas married John Rolfe, popular legend has it that she saved John Smith's life. Her father, Chief Powhatan, intended to kill the leader of the Jamestown colony. Smith was told to kneel and place his head on a large stone. Two huge Indians wielding heavy clubs were then ordered to smash his skull. History records that Pocahontas threw herself between Captain Smith and the club-bearing Indians and pleaded with her father to spare his life. According to legend, he did.

Organize this skit around the story of John Smith's ordeal and last-minute rescue.

SKIT 4—Indians Observing the Arrival of the *Mayflower* in 1621

Can you picture the thoughts of the Wampanoag Indians as they peered from the forest and saw the *Mayflower* as it approached?

In this skit, portray the reaction and possible conversation between the Indians as they watched the *Mayflower* land.

From Everyday Life: Colonial Times, published by Good Year Books. © 1997 Walter A. Hazen.

CHAPTER 11

Life on the Frontier

The frontier is where the developed part of a country ends and the wild, untamed part begins. America's first frontier began at the foothills of the Appalachian Mountains. These eastern mountains extend southwest from Canada to central Alabama. Later, as our nation grew, the frontier moved west to the Mississippi River and then on to the Rocky Mountains.

Pioneers moving west. Pioneers traveled in groups for protection. From a woodcut of 1874.

Most early colonists were content to settle along the Atlantic seaboard. There was plenty of land available, and there was safety in numbers. But as time passed, new arrivals found less land for their taking. Those who desired a few acres on which to farm were forced to settle farther inland. There were also hardy souls who valued their privacy and preferred to live apart from others. Daniel Boone, who grew up near the end of the colonial period, was one such person. Legend tells us that when he could see the smoke from the chimney of his nearest neighbor, he declared it was time to move on.

The first order of business on the frontier was to build some kind of shelter. Lean-tos and dugouts were used until a permanent cabin could be built of logs. As discussed in Chapter 2, the log cabin was not an American creation. It was brought to these shores by the Swedes and Germans who established the first frontier in parts of Delaware, New Jersey, and Pennsylvania. In time it became synonymous with the frontier and later the West.

Once a site was selected for a cabin, the first task was to cut down enough trees for its construction. All limbs and branches were removed, and logs were cut to lengths of 16 to 18 feet. The logs were notched at each end so they would fit together to make walls. Any gaps between logs were chinked, or filled with mud or clay. Windows and a door were sawn out once the walls

From *Everyday Life: Colonial Times*, published by Good Year Books. © 1997 Walter A. Hazen.

were in place. Like the colonists who settled in towns along the coast, frontier people had no glass for windows. Windows were covered with either animal skins or oiled paper. Many cabins also did not have floors. Those that did had floors made of puncheons. A puncheon floor was made from split logs arranged with the flat side upward. The flat surface of the logs were made as splinterless as possible with an ax.

Puncheons were also used to make tables, benches, and stools. Holes were made in the underside of the puncheons and pegs driven in for legs. Except for possibly a cradle, this was all the furniture the frontier family needed. A few made beds of poles built into the walls. For mattresses, they used dried grass or corn husks. Some settlers did not even bother with building beds; they simply rolled up in a blanket and slept on the floor.

The inside of a typical frontier home. All activities were carried out in a room that measured about ten feet by sixteen feet (3m × 5m).

In dress, the first pioneers imitated the Indians. Men wore a loose hunting shirt made of deerskin. The shirt was held in place by a belt on which hung the hunter's knife, tomahawk, and bullet bag. The shirt hung low over a pair of deerskin trousers. On his head, the early frontiersman wore a raccoon cap, and he covered his feet with a pair of moccasins. Because deerskin is not comfortable, the pioneer wore an inner shirt and underwear made of linsey-woolsey. Linsey-woolsey is a coarse cloth made of linen and wool or of cotton and wool. It was the material frontier women used to make their own clothing (see the illustration p. 88).

Frontier children dressed in the same manner as their parents. But unfortunately, they often went without shoes of any kind, even in winter. Boys and girls walked barefoot to school along frosty paths. Sometimes, before leaving home, they heated a board in the fireplace. They took the board with them when they started for school. When their feet became numb along the way, they stopped for a moment and stood on the board to warm their toes. Those children lucky enough to have moccasins often stuffed them with leaves or straw for added warmth.

From Everyday Life: Colonial Times, published by Good Year Books. © 1997 Walter A. Hazen.

Frontier people were a rough and simple breed. They cared little for the finer things of life. Their freedom and independence were foremost in their lives. Although friendly and hospitable, they did not tolerate any kind of lawbreaking. Thieving was dealt with swiftly and harshly. There were no pillories or stocks or jails on the frontier. A thief was lashed to a tree and flogged with a hickory rod. Afterwards, he returned to his work and the incident was considered closed.

A frontier woman weaves linsey-woolsey, a fabric made of linen and wool or cotton and wool. Because wool was limited, linen or cotton thread was woven together with wool thread to make it go farther.

Arguments between two rough frontiersmen were often settled with fists—and worse. Gouging, biting, and kicking seemed to have been an accepted part of the fight. Sometimes matters got completely out of hand and one or both combatants resorted to knives or axes. Since there were no courts, anyone who killed another person in a fight often went unpunished.

Frontier people were boisterous and rowdy. Weddings were lively affairs where every attempt was made to embarrass the newlyweds. Since competition was keen on the frontier, people liked to gather for running, jumping, and wrestling contests every chance they got. They also competed in shooting arrows and throwing tomahawks. Any activity that lent itself to competition appealed to frontiersmen.

In spite of their rough nature, frontier folk were hospitable and helpful. A stranger was never turned away from a door. And when a newcomer began to build a cabin, neighbors gathered from miles around for a "cabin raisin'." When the work was done, much eating and socializing followed.

Although the colonial period ended with America's independence from Great Britain, there were frontiersmen and pioneers for at least another century. The frontier period did not end until the American West was settled and tamed. But even afterwards, there were always people who sought the freedom and solitude of wide-open spaces.

The frontier has not completely disappeared. Perhaps it never will. Today's frontier is outer space. There are still adventurous souls who want to know what lies beyond the next hill or valley—or, as is the case today, the next galaxy.

From *Everyday Life: Colonial Times*, published by Good Year Books. © 1997 Walter A. Hazen.

Name _____ Date _____

Arrange in Chronological Order

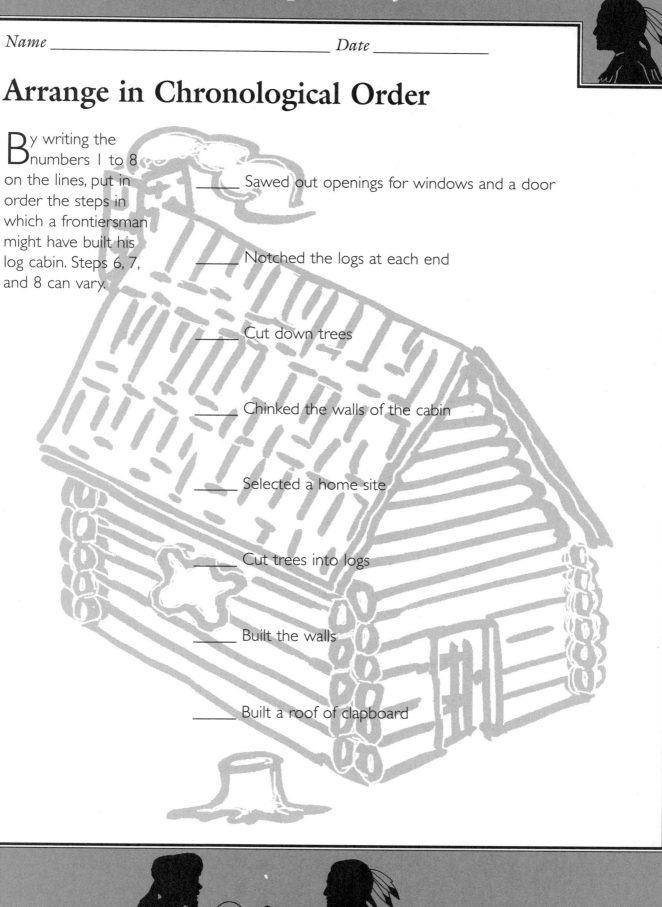

By writing the numbers 1 to 8 on the lines, put in order the steps in which a frontiersman might have built his log cabin. Steps 6, 7, and 8 can vary.

_____ Sawed out openings for windows and a door

_____ Notched the logs at each end

_____ Cut down trees

_____ Chinked the walls of the cabin

_____ Selected a home site

_____ Cut trees into logs

_____ Built the walls

_____ Built a roof of clapboard

Name _____ Date _____

Make a Frontier Diorama

Make a shoebox diorama or draw a mural depicting a scene from frontier life. You may want to look through books to get ideas.

Draw a plan for your diorama below. List the materials you'll need.

Materials needed:

_____   _____

_____   _____

_____   _____

_____   _____

From *Everyday Life: Colonial Times*, published by Good Year Books. © 1997 Walter A. Hazen.

Name _____ Date _____

Create a Dialogue About Frontier Life

Thomas Fletcher and his wife, Sarah, have just arrived in the colonies from England. When they learn that land is scarce and the prospects of acquiring a farm are bleak, they discuss the possibility of moving on to the frontier. Their children, Jeremiah and Naomi, are excited about the idea. Sarah Fletcher, however, is not sure if that is the best thing to do.

On the lines at right, create a dialogue involving the entire family discussing the pros and cons of life on the frontier.

From *Everyday Life: Colonial Times,* published by Good Year Books. © 1997 Walter A. Hazen.

Name _____ Date _____

Write a Letter About Wilderness Life

Imagine that you are living in colonial New England and you have gone to visit your cousins, Jeb and Rachel, who live with their parents in a log cabin on the frontier in Kentucky. You naturally have found life there very exciting and quite different, and you are eager to write home and tell all about it.

On the lines at right, write a letter to your Mom and Dad— or someone else at home— relating your experiences and giving your impressions of life in the wilderness.

Date_____

Dear _____,

_____

_____

_____

_____

_____

_____

_____

_____

_____

_____

_____

_____

_____

_____

_____

_____

_____

_____

Love,

_____

From *Everyday Life: Colonial Times*, published by Good Year Books. © 1997 Walter A. Hazen.

Answers to Activities

Chapter 1

Common Colonial Illnesses

Typhoid Fever   Cause: a bacillus found in food and water where poor sanitation exists. Symptoms: fever, headache and pains, nausea, red spots on body. Prevention: good personal hygiene and public sanitation.

Malaria   Cause: a parasite spread by the bite of mosquitoes. Symptoms: chills, fever, sweating, weakness. Treatment: drugs such as quinine.

Smallpox   Cause: a virus that is usually spread by coughing, sneezing, etc. Symptoms: chills, headache, pains in back and limbs, fever, nausea, red spots on skin. Prevention: vaccination.

Diphtheria   Cause: a bacteria that attacks the throat. Symptoms: fever, sore throat, swollen neck glands. Treatment: large doses of antitoxin. Prevention: sanitary measures, inoculation.

Scarlet Fever   Cause: streptococcus bacteria. Symptoms: fever, nausea, headaches, muscle pains, skin rash. Treatment: isolation of patient to prevent spread, penicillin and other drugs.

Measles   Cause: a virus spread by coughing and sneezing. Symptoms: fever, cough, runny nose, sensitive eyes, small pink spots all over. Prevention: vaccination.

Distinguish Fact and Opinion— Facts: families were large; parents were very strict. Opinions: there were never any arguments; parents cared more for their children than parents do today; children were not very happy in those days.

Chapter 2

Prove Your Math Skills—1. 224 square feet; 2a. Town B; 2b. Town D; 2c. Towns A and C

Chapter 3

Try Some Wig Math— a. $16; b. $48; c. $56

Increase Your Fashion Vocabulary

1. doublet—a man's close-fitting jacket
2. breeches—short trousers fastened at the knees
3. waistcoat —a man's vest
4. stays—strips of whalebone used to stiffen women's corsets and collars
5. cravat—a wide necktie
6. neckcloth—a starched, white collar worn by women in colonial New England

From *Everyday Life: Colonial Times*, published by Good Year Books. © 1997 Walter A. Hazen.

7. whalebone—an elastic substance obtained from the upper jaws of whales and used to stiffen corsets and dresses
8. ruff—a high, frilled, stiff collar worn by men in the sixteenth and seventeenth centuries
9. petticoat—a skirt worn beneath a dress or outer skirt

Chapter 4

Find Which Word Does Not Belong

1. trencher; a trencher was not made of iron and was not a cooking utensil
2. pumpkin; a pumpkin is a fruit; the others are vegetables
3. tea; tea is not an alcoholic beverage
4. oysters; oysters are not fish
5. rabbit; a rabbit is not a bird or fowl
6. squash; a squash is a vegetable
7. evening; evening is not a meal
8. crab; a crab is a seafood
9. molasses; molasses is not made from milk

Solve a Food Crossword

Across 3. hasty 5. olijkoeck
    7. samp 9. trencher 12. venison

Down 1. water 2. grits 4. corn
    6. mutton 8. porridge 10. cod
    11. Boston

Chapter 5

Solve a Word Problem

Group B shucked 378 ears. Total number of ears shucked was 728.

Interpret a Line Graph

1. 8 2. 4 3. Anne; John 4. 6

Chapter 6

Solve Some Dame School Math

1. 40% 2. 3 3. 6 4. 6 5. 80%

Chapter 7

Name That Craftsman

1. cooper 2. blacksmith
3. whitesmith 4. cobbler 5. tailor
6. cabinetmaker 7. sawyer
8. chandler 9. tinker 10. potter

Find the Main Idea

Answers will vary, but should be similar to the following:

Paragraph 1: People in America were never equal.

Paragraph 3: Orphaned children sometimes became indentured servants.

Paragraph 5: Hard work and ability determined social status in America.

Paragraph 9: New England farms were small.

Paragraph 11: Overseers supervised plantations for absentee owners.

Paragraph 19: Young men learned a trade by becoming an apprentice.

From *Everyday Life: Colonial Times*, published by Good Year Books. © 1997 Walter A. Hazen.

Roll Out the Barrel

1. 126 quarts; 504 quarts; 6 pints
2. 6 hogsheads; 12 barrels
3. 39.36 bushels

Compare Cities Then and Now

1. They were dangerous; there was always the threat of crime; they were dirty, as are some cities today.
2. Animals freely roamed the streets; fires were frequent; sanitation facilities were poor.

Chapter 8

Solve Some Math Traveling Problems

1. 30 miles or 48 kilometers
2. 52 miles or 84 kilometers per hour
3. 24-1/4 days

Compare and Contrast Two Eras

Answers will vary, but should be similar to the following:

Travel: Colonial Times—walking; horseback; boat; stagecoach
Today—automobiles; airplanes; railroads

Lodging: Colonial Times—widely-scattered inns
Today—motels; hotels

Postal Service: Colonial Times—slow, infrequent, usually on horseback
Today—regular mail delivery; airborne express, and so forth

Communication: Colonial Times—very few newspapers; news often spread by towncriers. Today—widespread newspapers; radio; television; computer networks

Chapter 9

Test Your Medical Vocabulary—

young; doctors; medical; quacks; patients; ingredients; bewitched; natural; diseases; prevented; sanitation; immunized; survive; antibiotics; deaths.

Solve a Medicine Crossword

Across   1. fleam   3. vapors   5. fever
8. blacksmith   9. rabies
11. opium

Down   2. leech   4. phlebotomy
6. Endicott   7. king   9. rum
10. five

Chapter 10

Interpret a Bar Graph

1. 68 thousand
2. about 24%
3. 7 thousand
4. 37 thousand
5. about 13%

Chapter 11

Arrange in Chronological Order

6, 4, 2, 7, 1, 3, 5, 8

From *Everyday Life: Colonial Times*, published by Good Year Books. © 1997 Walter A. Hazen.

Additional Resources

Books for Children

Bial, Raymond. *Frontier Home.* Boston: Houghton Mifflin Company, 1993.

Earle, Alice Morse. *Home Life in Colonial Days.* Middle Village, NY: Jonathan David Publishers, 1975.

Farquhar, Margaret C. *Colonial Life in America.* New York: Holt, Rinehart and Winston, 1962.

Fradin, Dennis B. *The Massachusetts Colony.* Chicago: Childrens Press, 1987.

Kellen, Stuart. *Life in the Thirteen Colonies.* Minneapolis: Abdo & Daughters, 1990.

Madison, Arnold. *How the Colonists Lived.* New York: David McKay Company, Inc., 1981.

Palmer, Ann. *Growing Up in Colonial America.* East Sussex, England: Wayland Publishers Limited, 1979.

Sherrow, Victoria. *Huskings, Quiltings, and Barn Raisings: Work-Play Parties in Early America.* New York: Walker and Company, 1992.

Terkel, Susan Neiburg. *Colonial American Medicine.* New York: Franklin Watts, 1993.

Warner, John F. *Colonial American Home Life.* New York: Franklin Watts, 1993.

Books for Adults

Earle, Alice Morse. *Child Life in Colonial Days.* Stockbridge, Massachusetts: Berkshire House Publishers, 1993.

Tunis, Edwin. *Colonial Living.* New York: Thomas Y. Crowell, 1957.

——*Frontier Living.* New York: Thomas Y. Crowell, 1961.

——*The Young United States.* New York: World Publishing Co., 1969.

From *Everyday Life: Colonial Times*, published by Good Year Books. © 1997 Walter A. Hazen.

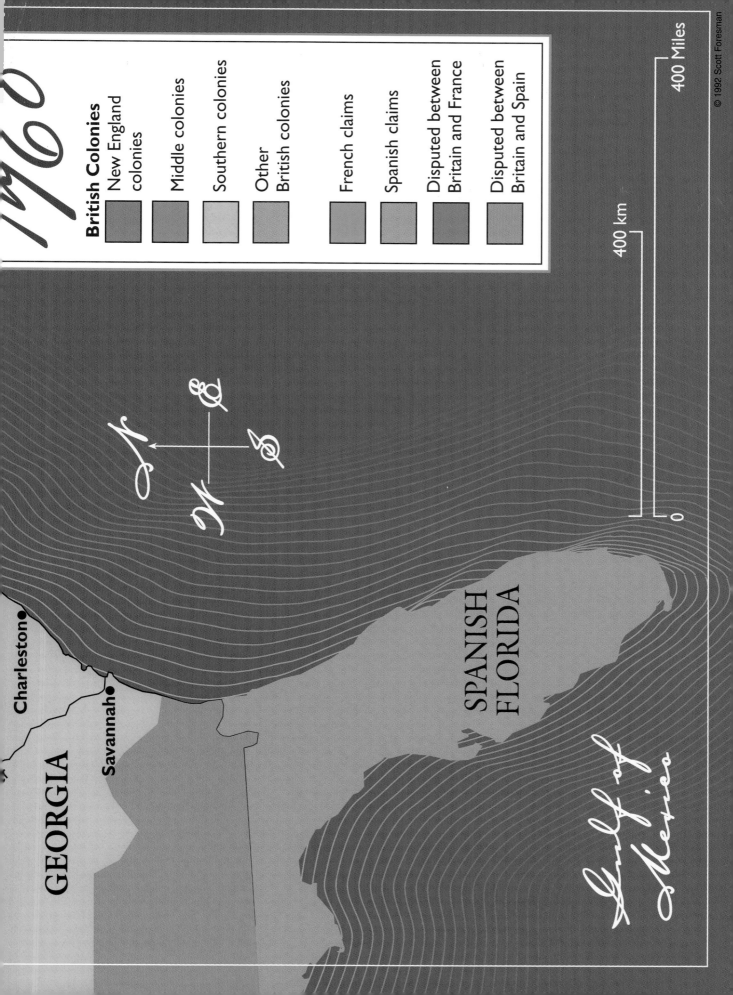

1760

British Colonies

New England colonies

Middle colonies

Southern colonies

Other British colonies

French claims

Spanish claims

Disputed between Britain and France

Disputed between Britain and Spain

400 km

400 Miles

0

N W S E

GEORGIA

Charleston

Savannah

SPANISH FLORIDA

Gulf of Mexico

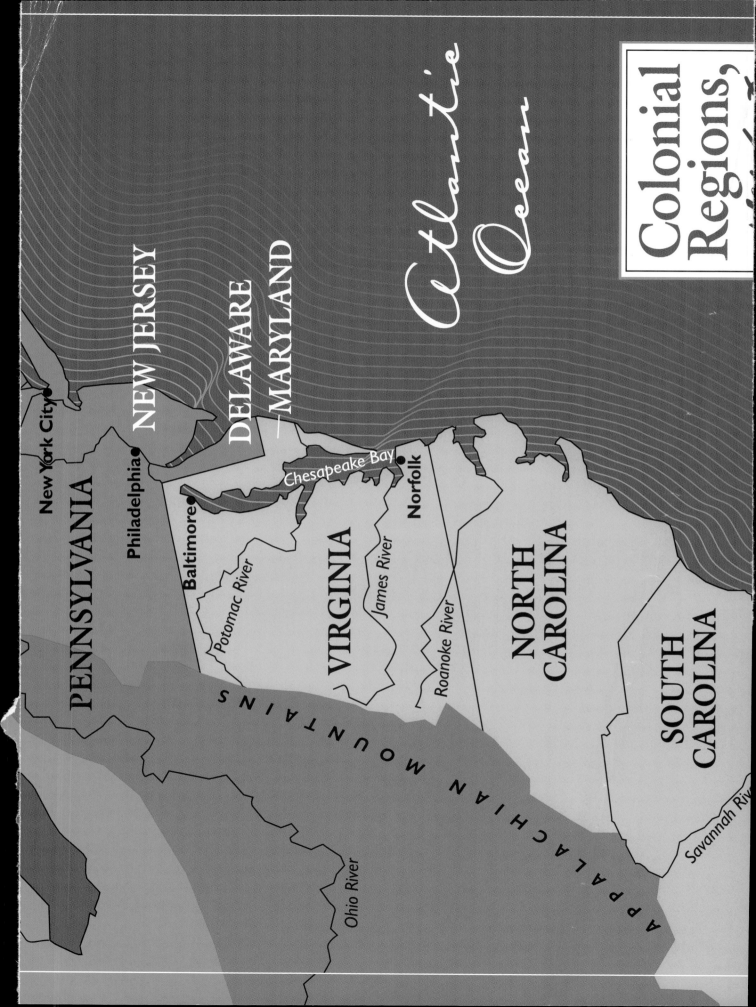

Colonial Regions,

Atlantic Ocean

New York City•
PENNSYLVANIA
Philadelphia•
NEW JERSEY
Baltimore•
DELAWARE
MARYLAND
Potomac River
VIRGINIA
James River
Chesapeake Bay
Norfolk•
Roanoke River
NORTH CAROLINA
SOUTH CAROLINA
APPALACHIAN MOUNTAINS
Ohio River
Savannah Riv

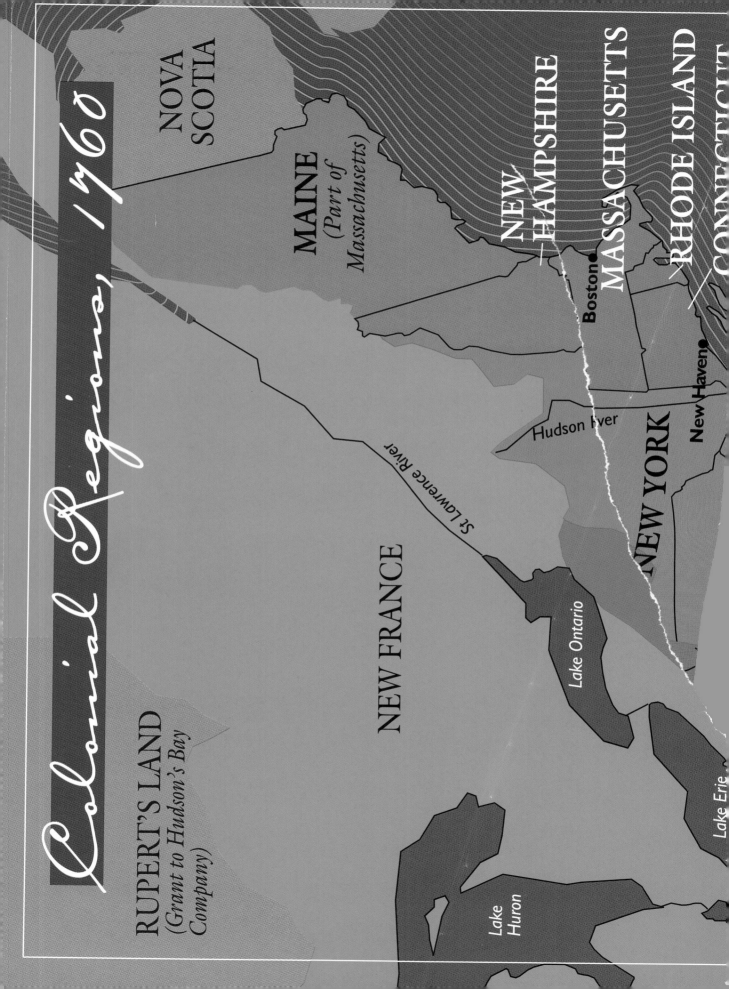

Colonial Regions, 1760

RUPERT'S LAND
(Grant to Hudson's Bay Company)

NOVA SCOTIA

MAINE
(Part of Massachusetts)

NEW HAMPSHIRE

MASSACHUSETTS

RHODE ISLAND

CONNECTICUT

Boston

NEW YORK

New Haven

Hudson River

St Lawrence River

NEW FRANCE

Lake Ontario

Lake Erie

Lake Huron